POSTERS

OF

WORLD WAR TWO

POSTERS

OF
WORLD WAR
TWO

DENIS JUDD

ST. MARTIN'S PRESS · NEW YORK

AFFILIATED PUBLISHERS: Macmillan Limited, London—
also at Bombay, Calcutta, Madras and Melbourne

Contents

Preface

A huge number of war posters were issued between the late 1930s and 1945, representing the hopes, fears and ambitions of many nations. This volume presents one selection from the vast stock of material available, and re-produces many which have remained unpublished since the war years. The final choice of posters is meant to give the reader a chance of comparing different national styles as well as helping to illuminate certain vital aspects of the war. A large part of the text tries to describe and analyze the progress of the war as an essential background to the posters but fundamentally, of course, the posters speak eloquently for themselves, and this, in most cases, is enough.

I owe many debts of gratitude as a result of preparing this book. My friend Stuart Durant put his considerable specialist knowledge at my disposal in considering the graphic qualities of the posters. If the last part of the book, on the graphics of the posters, has any value it is due largely to him. I had a most imaginative and persistent picture researcher in Linda Cicalese. Among those who translated various captions for me I am particularly grateful to Dr. Hugh Baker of the School of Oriental and African Studies, London, and to Sue Branney, Elizabeth Klotchkoff and Nora Boomsluiter of the Polytechnic of North London. Frances Smith typed certain sections of the book with great speed and efficiency. Finally, the patience of my publishers has only been equalled by that of my wife and children.

Denis Judd
London, 1971

Note on references. A plate is referred to in the text by the number of the section in which it appears (or 'C' if it is in the colour section) followed by the number of the particular plate.

Introduction

THE WAR IN EUROPE

Origins

From SEPTEMBER, 1939, to December, 1941, the Second World War was fought solely between the European powers. Great Britain, however, was supported by her Dominions and her Empire, and the Free French hoped to carry on the struggle from the French colonies in Africa after the fall of France. Not until the Japanese attack on Pearl Harbour in December, 1941, did the war widen into a global struggle, a real world war. Previously even the theatres of the land war had been confined to Europe, and to North Africa on the other side of the Mediterranean. At sea the Royal Navy had struggled to maintain control of the Atlantic and Indian Oceans, as well as the Mediterranean and home waters.

The irruption of Japan and the United States into the war changed all this, just as Hitler's attack on Soviet Russia in June, 1941, had brought to an end the gruelling twelve months in which Britain had stood alone against Germany and her allies. Suddenly the vast Pacific had to be taken into account, the old European imperial order in south-east Asia was torn down, the frontiers of British India were no longer secure.

What caused the European powers to go to war in the first place? The deeper pressures can be readily discerned, even if not all observers would agree about their relative importance. Fundamental, however, were the grievances and discontents of the German people. Humiliated by the Versailles Peace Treaty of 1919, stripped of territory, saddled with debts, forbidden the rearmament necessary to great power status, post war Germany had cause to look back to the departed glories of the Wilhelmine Empire with bitterness and regret.

The Nazi movement had flourished on such discontent. The catastrophic results of the Great Depression had heightened the social crisis. With millions of Germans unemployed, and the deutsch mark subject to wild deflation, successive governments of the Weimar Republic had failed both to find economic solutions, and to assert an acceptable degree of national sovereignty. Although before 1933 Hitler had shown that he was not above brutality, and despite the bizarre quality of a good deal of his party's propaganda, he had achieved the Chancellorship by legitimate means. Once he was in power, however, he set about smashing his opponents and turning political convention upside down.

The early years of Hitler's rule did not horrify all onlookers. To some, national socialism was not easily distinguishable from populism or guild-socialism. To others, Hitler's violent opposition to bolshevism made him a bulwark against the "red threat" from the east. Nor did it seem unreasonable that the new German government should express its open dislike of the Versailles Treaty which had emasculated a once proud and warlike nation.

The Nazis had also managed to bring about a substantial improvement in Germany's economic life, just as Mussolini had grappled, sometimes merely for histrionic effect, with domestic Italian problems.

Of course there were growing moral qualms as Hitler proceeded to turn Germany from a democratic into a totalitarian country. The suppression of rival political parties, the introduction of the concentration camps, the state control of propaganda and the means of mass communication, were disturbing phenomena. Yet they were not unique in recent European experience. Critics of Soviet Russia accused her of similar conduct. Throughout the world there were few states who enjoyed a system of government comparable with the "Westminster model". International trade required stability, not democracy. Fascism was not yet accepted universally as a dirty word.

The Nazis' treatment of the Jews, however, was much more difficult to swallow. Here again, anti-semitism was as old as the Diaspora. Tsarist Russia had indulged in fearsome pogroms; contemporary Polish attitudes left a great deal to be desired. Probably some anti-semitic feeling lurked in many Gentile breasts. But the character of the Nazi campaign against the Jews, the mindless brutality, the gross public humiliations, were repellent and beyond excuse. Furthermore, contact with Jewish refugees, who included distinguished academics, musicians, scientists and doctors, as well as bankers and business men, did much to harden opinion against the regime which had persecuted them.

The repugnant qualities of Nazi Germany were not the real causes of the war but they certainly strengthened the resolve of Germany's enemies once fighting had broken out. An anti-fascist crusade was attractive to communists and many others on the Left, but the staider governments of Britain, France and the United States were not anxious to take up this particular sword. Soviet Russia was the country most ideologically opposed to fascism, but failing to find sufficient formal backing in western Europe, Stalin seemed to turn prevailing antagonism on its head when he signed the Non-Aggression Pact with Hitler in 1939.

Did Hitler plan a great war of conquest? Certainly he coveted the *Lebensraum* (or "living space") to the east. To have the Ukraine as a granary for the ever-expanding Third Reich, to use the Slav people as the slave labour force for the German *herrenvolk*, were attractive aims. In order to attack the Soviet Union, however, Germany would have to pass through eastern Europe. Hungary and Rumania, in the event, were enthusiastic allies for an assault on bolshevist Russia, but Czechoslovakia and Poland were real obstacles. Hitler planned to conquer these two awkward Slav states. Probably he hoped to avoid war with Britain and France, and saw no reason why the isolationist United States need be drawn in to any European crisis. After all, his plans would hardly have included a struggle against the grand alliance of the British Empire, Russia and the United States. Suicide in a Berlin bunker was not the chosen fate of the Fuhrer of the Third Reich.

German grievances and ambitions might have been contained by resolute and sensible international action in the interwar years. But the founders of the League of Nations were soon to have their hopes dashed, and individual nations only occasionally attempted to guarantee the new frontiers of Europe. The Locarno Treaty of 1925 (between Germany, France and Belgium) was an essay in non-aggression, but the "Locarno spirit" did not catch on generally. The principle of disarmament was undoubtedly acceptable to the victorious powers in 1918, yet there was no effective control of disarmament. After Hitler rose to power Germany began to re-arm, and this in turn caused uneasiness among other nations and a noisy demand for rearmament from some quarters.

The disinclination of Great Britain and France to go to war to stop Hitler led to the policy of appeasement. In order to buy off Germany, the British and French governments were even prepared to sell Czech independence. The Munich agreement of 1938 did just this. The Anglo-French guarantees offered subsequently to Poland were no more than half-hearted assurances, lacking the clear means of fulfilment. Hitler was not bought off by appeasement; nor was he alarmed by the Anglo-French guarantees to Poland.

In March, 1939, Czechoslovakia–stripped of its Sudetenland defences by the Munich agreement–was dismembered. Slovakia became an independent state, Hungary laid hands on coveted border lands, and the apparatus of Nazi totalitarianism was established over the ancient province of Bohemia. The destruction of Czechoslovakia was more or less predictable but, for all that, reaction in Britain, and even in France, was sharp. Hitler had thrown off the sheepskin and stood revealed as a ravening wolf. He had to be stopped.

The triumphant sound of jackboots in the streets of Prague led to Britain and France guaranteeing Poland. To strengthen their undertaking an alliance with the Soviet Union would have been most desirable. However, no such alliance was made. Perhaps both the British and the French governments harboured suspicions of bolshevism that were too deep-rooted to be exorcised even by the Nazi threat. Maybe Russia underestimated (with good reason) the new resolve of Britain and France. At any rate in August, 1939, Molotov and Ribbentrop signed the Nazi-Soviet Pact.

After some days of diplomatic scuffling, German troops invaded Poland on 1st September. The *Luftwaffe* bombed Warsaw (11.11). For a short time the British government's response was uncertain. The Cabinet toyed with the idea of yet another conference but the House of Commons would have none of it. Not only Labour and Liberal members, but also the bulk of the Conservative Party in the House, now demanded war. Chamberlain gave way. On 3rd September, 1939, an ultimatum was issued to the German government at 9 a.m. It expired two hours later.

France followed Britain into the war. The British Dominions made up their own minds. Australia and New Zealand were dragged in by the twin pull of apron strings and the umbilical cord that still connected them to the Mother Country. The Canadian Parliament assented to war on 10th September. (C.34). In South Africa General Smuts, both out of conviction and an anxiety for power, supported a declaration of war. The Parliament at Cape Town voted for war by a slender margin, and Smuts became Prime Minister. The Irish Free State, a reluctant Dominion member of the British Empire, preferred to remain neutral; thus the ghosts of the 1916 Sinn Fein rebels gained revenge from their graves. India and the dependent Empire were automatically committed to the war by Britain's entry, but it was questionable whether India would play as loyal a supporting role as in 1914. Despite such doubts, the British Empire confronted Germany for the second time in twenty years.

The Phoney War (1939-1940)

At first nothing seemed to happen. German troops continued the drive into Poland from the west, while Russian forces invaded from the east—a reasonable precaution, though much criticised in Britain and France. But the *Luftwaffe* did not swoop upon London or Paris. The French army did not plunge across the Rhine. Having declared war because of Germany's violation of Poland, Britain and France stood by while their eastern ally was brutally dismembered.

On the British home front plans made before the outbreak of war were adhered to. A million and a half primary schoolchildren and mothers with children under five years old were evacuated from urban areas most threatened by air attack (5.1). A blackout was imposed which was inconvenient and even hazardous, especially on the roads. Millions of gas masks were issued; these at least provided children with exotic toys throughout the war (5.5). But the bombs did not fall as anticipated. The prophecies of writers like H. G. Wells were, for the moment, unfulfilled.

In the government a certain amount of reshuffling took place. Chamberlain brought Winston Churchill out of the political wilderness and appointed him First Lord of the Admiralty, an office he had held in the first months of the Great War. Anthony Eden became Dominions' Secretary. New ministries were set up to deal with the urgent business of modern warfare—food, supply, shipping, information and propaganda, security and labour. But Chamberlain's War Cabinet bore an uncanny resemblance to the old Cabinet of the appeasement era. The Prime Minister himself was hardly cast in the mould of Chatham or Lloyd George, and indeed did not aspire to be.

The "Phoney War" was named so because it was strangely quiet and peaceful. Military conscription lumbered on. The R.A.F. contented itself with dropping not bombs, but ineffective propaganda leaflets on the citizens of the Third Reich. A British Expeditionary Force crossed to France and took up positions on the French frontier with Belgium. The large and well-equipped French army crouched behind the apparently inviolable Maginot line. It was not even possible for the allies to attack Italy in North Africa or Abyssinia, since Mussolini had declared that he was a non-belligerent.

To some extent, furious effort did not seem necessary. The German economy was supposed to be weak and some expected it to crack under the strain of war. The Royal Navy's blockade of Germany would hasten this decline. Perhaps the British and French government still hoped that they could negotiate a reasonable peace with Hitler: a free hand for Germany in eastern Europe might be traded for the maintenance of the British Empire. Certainly the allied countries needed time to build up their war machines and establish a war economy. In Britain the government introduced food rationing, and warily raised the level of income tax (to $37\frac{1}{2}$ per cent) and some indirect taxes. As yet, however, the industrial life of the nation was still geared to peacetime requirements. There was no wholesale redirection of labour or of production. As late as May, 1940, the munitions industry was undermanned by 80 per cent.

Only at sea did the nation seem truly at war (1.2). The German U-boats preyed heavily on allied merchant shipping, and even hit the Royal Navy hard. In September, 1939, they sank the aircraft carrier *Courageous*, and later they attacked the great naval base at Scapa Flow and sank the battleship *Royal Oak*. Equally dramatic were the daring raids of the German pocket battleships. One of these, the *Graf Spee*, terrorised the South Atlantic until resolutely harried by three smaller British ships, who forced her into Montevideo harbour where she scuttled herself on the Führer's orders. Thus, despite the thousands of tons of British merchant shipping sent to the bottom of the Atlantic, the great days of Nelson and Jervis seemed to live on.

Elsewhere the allied war effort turned to ashes. In November, 1939, Russia invaded Finland in order to promote her security in the Baltic. The Finns resisted heroically and successfully. An Anglo-French expeditionary force was formed to land at Narvik on the Norwegian coast and then to cross to Finland via Norway and Sweden. It was a shoddily executed plan. Finland made peace with Russia before the allies could move. Hitler invaded Denmark and Norway in April, 1940. Belatedly the allies captured Narvik, and were then forced to withdraw. The German conquest of Denmark and Norway was completed.

The humiliations of the Narvik campaign swept Neville Chamberlain out of 10 Downing Street and Winston Churchill became Prime Minister of a Wartime Coalition government in May, 1940. Still distrusted by many Conservative M.P.'s, still capable of rash and impulsive action, Churchill seemed nevertheless the man for the times (2.2). Labour and Liberals were prepared to serve under him; and he was probably the people's choice. At any rate, he dedicated himself to his forbidding task in heroic and defiant terms. On his first appearance in the House of Commons as Prime Minister, he declared: "I have nothing to offer but blood, toil, tears and sweat. You ask, What is our policy? I will say: It is to wage war, by sea, land, and air, with all the strength that God can give us . . . You ask, What is our aim? I can answer in one word: Victory—victory at all costs, victory in spite of all terror; victory, however long and hard the road might be."

The Blitzkreig and "Their Finest Hour" (1940-1941)

The immediate aftermath of Churchill's accession to supreme power was characterised by defeat rather than victory. On 10th May German troops smashed into Belgium and the Netherlands. Although allied forces moved against them it was of no avail. The Netherlands army surrendered on 15th May; Rotterdam was heavily bombed. Queen Wilhemina set up a government-in-exile in London. Simultaneously the German panzer division punched a hole through the allied defences on the Belgian border and in a few days reached the English Channel.

The war strategy of the allies was ruined in one stroke. The expensive complexities of the Maginot Line were useless, since the German army, had simply gone round the end of the Line! Huge French forces were cut off from any useful part in the battle. The British Expeditionary Force fought a retreat to the Belgian coast. There, at Dunkirk, something was snatched from the catastrophe of defeat. Sheltered by the R.A.F. (a fact not appreciated by many who fought on the beaches) and the Royal Navy, the vast majority of the B.E.F., as well as nearly 140,000 French troops, were brought back to Britain. True, they had lost their equipment, but they had not lost their lives. Later, even more allied troops were saved. In all, 558,000 men were rescued during the Fall of France, of whom 368,000 were British.

The success of Dunkirk could not, however, disguise the magnitude of the allied disaster. France, with her ancient martial traditions, with all her culture and intellectual excellence, had been ripped apart. In June, Churchill tried a last fling to keep the French fighting. He offered an indissoluble union between Britain and France. There seemed little in it for the French. German troops had goose-stepped along the Champs-Elysées, the French soldier was not inclined, perhaps understandably, to fight to the bitter end. Marshall Pétain, the hero of Verdun, formed a government and asked for peace. On 22nd June an armistice was concluded. Northern France and the coastline to the Pyrenees became occupied territory. The rest of the country, ruled from the quiet town of Vichy, received a spurious identity. The swastika flew on the Channel coast.

In Britain, somewhat amazingly, the mood of the people was defiant, even optimistic. The days of "splendid isolation" were not far distant. A popular mythology surrounded the defeat of the Spanish Armada, even the Napoleonic Wars. The value of "standing alone" was deeply entrenched in British tradition. A fortified island defended by a loyal and united people would be more than a match for the leader of the Third Reich and his armoured hordes (2.2). The Royal Navy would still rule the waves, the R.A.F. would doubtless rule the air. Help would come from the English-speaking

Dominions, eventually even from the United States. As Churchill promised, the British lion, her lion cubs at her side, would roar defiance at the Nazi eagle.

Facts did not always support such confidence. The victorious German army was a redoubtable opponent. The R.A.F. had suffered heavy losses during the Battle of France, and was outnumbered by the *Luftwaffe*. The economic resources of much of Europe were now at Hitler's command. Such help as the Dominions could send could hardly tilt the military balance; the United States professed neutrality. Britain's economy had still not been effectively geared to wartime needs, and the training of conscripts would take time.

Yet, inspired by Winston Churchill, the British people bravely prepared for battle. Churchill hit exactly the right note in his broadcasts to the nation. His speeches were belligerent and confident, full of rich symbolism and rotund phrases. He poured scorn on "Corporal Hitler" and all his gang, as well as on the "whipped running-dog" Mussolini, who had entered the war only when France came crashing down. In June, 1940, as Britain prepared itself for invasion, Churchill exhorted: "Let us therefore brace ourselves to our duties, and so bear ourselves that, if the British Empire and its Commonwealth last for a thousand years, men will still say: 'This was their finest hour.'"

Aircraft production was a key to survival – perhaps the only one worth concentrating on in mid-1940. Churchill appointed the dynamic press magnate Beaverbrook to the post of Minister of Aircraft Production. Beaverbrook soon had the aircraft factories working at full stretch. Members of the public also surrendered iron railings, gates and cooking utensils for scrap metal. Whether this made much difference to the production of Spitfires and Hurricanes is open to question, but it gave men and women the feeling that they were really contributing to the war effort. The formation of the Home Guard quickly involved more than a million men in part-time martial activities that were at least good for morale. The royal family set an impeccable example by their refusal to leave London for safer retreats.

Churchill tried to woo President Roosevelt into an alliance through an exchange of private and lengthy letters. After all, if the United States would support Britain when it mattered, then all might still be saved. Roosevelt could not yet renounce neutrality. Probably he had no pressing desire to do so. Of course, the British government could go shopping for American armaments, though these could not be paid for in dollars indefinitely. Roosevelt, nonetheless, did what he could. He sent half a million rifles for the scantily equipped Home Guard. Later, the United States traded in fifty middle-aged destroyers for bases in the British West Indian Islands and Newfoundland. The destroyers had, at the very least, a symbolic significance: perhaps more help would now come from the reluctant "arsenal of democracy".

The expected German invasion of Britain did not materialize. Anxious eyes scanned the skies for paratroops; across the Channel it was known that barges were assembling. Hitler probably hoped that he could still negotiate a peace with Britain, despite Churchill's rhetorical call for total victory. Certainly he had to reassure his generals that he would not launch an invasion until the *Luftwaffe* had established air superiority. Between July and September, 1940, he attempted just this.

The Battle of Britain was fought against the blue skies of an exceptionally fine English summer. Though short of reserves of trained pilots, Fighter Command was not short of first-rate aircraft – as long as losses were kept down. This was done. For propaganda purposes the number of German planes destroyed was exaggerated, but the ratio of losses was firmly in the R.A.F.'s favour. The new invention of radar helped the British cause, and for some reason the Germans did not knock out the radar stations. On 15th September the *Luftwaffe's* assault reached its climax. It was repulsed. Two days later Hitler decided to postpone the invasion of Britain (Operation Sea Lion) indefinitely.

Apart from the skilful and heroic efforts of the pilots of Fighter Command (rewarded by Churchill's judgment that "Never in the course of human conflict was so much owed by so many to so few"), the *Luftwaffe* had lost the Battle of Britain on strategical grounds. Instead of continuing to bomb Fighter Command's bases like Manston, Tangmere or Hawkinge, the Germans decided to attack London and other major industrial cities. This was mainly a retaliation against an R.A.F. raid on Berlin at the end of August, which was itself a retaliation for a relatively insignificant bombing of London earlier.

Despite the postponement of Operation Sea Lion, however, the Blitz grew in intensity. London was bombed for seventy-six nights in succession. In November a large part of industrial Coventry was obliterated. Other cities, some of no particular strategical significance, were attacked. Great fires, many caused by incendiary bombs, raged. Two out of every seven houses in Britain were destroyed or damaged. Thousands of Londoners took nightly refuge in Underground stations. Others sheltered in dug-outs in their gardens, or even crouched under kitchen tables. Total civilian losses in Britain during the war numbered about 60,000. A second flood of evacuees left the cities during the Blitz, adding to the population dislocation that resulted from thousands of homes being destroyed (5.2).

But though the flames licked around St. Paul's Cathedral, "London could take it." So could a score of lesser cities and towns, so indeed could the British people as a whole. Prewar fears that concentrated bombing would destroy civilian morale were ill-founded. Later the urban population of Germany showed as much stoicism as their British equivalents. Even when, towards the end of the war, the secret German weapons the V.1., and the V.2. plunged down on London the people's nerve held (1.11).

The Blitz did not even seriously disturb British industrial output. Factories were set up in rural areas, and even devastated Coventry was able to resume full production in less than a week. In some ways, the Blitz positively helped the British war effort. Civilians really were in the front line. Indeed until September, 1941, more civilians had been killed than fighting men. Common danger, the nightly alerts, fire-fighting and rescue operations, kindled a sense of unity. No class was exempt from the Blitz; although the mean terraces of the East End were shattered, so was Buckingham Palace and the House of Commons. Perhaps the people's will to fight the war through to the bitter finish was strengthened by the Blitz. Certainly when the House of Commons debated the possibilities of a negotiated peace in December, 1940, they rejected it by 341 to 4. Even when the German raids became much less frequent after the middle of 1941 the desire to pay back in kind did not abate.

During the Battle of Britain and the Blitz, Britain was engaged in an equally deadly war at sea. The Battle of the Atlantic pivoted on bringing the essential convoys home to British ports. As in the First World War, German U-boats caused havoc despite the convoy system. By learning to coordinate the protective roles of aircraft and warships, the British managed to stave off starvation and disaster. In 1941 the United States, though still neutral, began to patrol further out into the Atlantic. In May, 1941, the Royal Navy and the R.A.F. between them trapped and sank the powerful German battleship *Bismarck*.

The United States government took a further friendly step by introducing lend-lease in 1941. Under this system Britain did not have to pay cash for goods bought from America. This meant that despite the huge loans Britain was raising, she now had almost unlimited credit in the United States. With Russia and America still out of the war, the British government confidently took the offensive in several theatres. Bombing raids on Germany grew in intensity, even though they were far less effective than their advocates believed.

In the Mediterranean, British torpedoes had already sunk half the Italian fleet at Taranto. In East Africa, General Wavell threw the Italians out of Cyrenaica, taking 113,000 prisoners. Mussolini's discomfiture however, invoked a reluctant German intervention, not only in North Africa but also in Greece which Italy had invaded in October, 1940 (C.29). Greece fell to the Germans, as did the Island of Crete, despite British intervention. In North Africa, German troops under General Rommel pushed the British back to the borders of Egypt. It seemed as if the British Empire had hardly begun the long climb towards victory, if indeed it could ever succeed at all unaided.

But in June, 1941, Germany invaded Soviet Russia. The Nazi-Soviet pact of 1939 had bought Russia nearly two years of useful non-belligerence. Stalin had half-expected Hitler to attack in 1941, but when it came, the invasion staggered the Russians with its force and violence (2.42). Three million confident German troops poured across the Soviet border, breaking deep into Russian territory. The *Luftwaffe* swooped down on Russian air bases, while German tank columns scattered the Red Army. By December the German armies had penetrated within nineteen miles of Moscow, were beseiging Leningrad in the north, and had taken Stalingrad and Kharkov in the south. The *Wermacht's* great drive to the east had brought the Ukraine under German rule. Kiev had fallen, yielding half a million prisoners-of-war to the victors. Indeed the early successes of the invasion had left German troops exhausted with the speed of their advance. Motorised detachments ploughed on over the dusty roadways, while marches of twenty-five miles per day were not unusual for foot soldiers.

Yet despite the position of the battle line in December, 1941, the Germans had not fulfilled the original objectives of operation "Barbarossa". By autumn the advance should have engulfed Leningrad and Moscow and reached the northern port of Archangel and the Volga river in the south. Even the staggering early success of "Barbarossa" involved serious disadvantages. Although the Ukraine had been occupied, the atrocities of the S.S. and other detachments meant that those of the local populace who might have collaborated with the invaders were permanently antagonised. Hundreds of thousands of civilians starved to death (2.41). Few of the 3,000,000 Russian troops captured in 1941 survived. Frequently they were left in hastily built prisoner-of-war camps to die of hunger and disease.

The bestiality of German forces in occupied Russia ensured that henceforth Soviet troops would fight to the death rather than surrender (9.5). The partisans harried German communications, often at terrible cost to themselves. Since, in accordance with Nazi preconceptions, the Ukraine was treated as one vast slave labour camp, the slaves were only too eager to cut the throats of their masters when opportunity arose.

Despite the opposition, by December, 1941, Hitler's empire stretched from the Channel to the gates of Leningrad, and from the Baltic to the Black Sea (9.1). Although Britain had hastened to ally herself with Soviet Russia, her new partner seemed to be a helpless giant stricken with the deadliest of foes. Then on 7th December, 1941, Japanese carrier-based planes swooped down on the American naval base at Pearl Harbour, destroying a large part of the Pacific Fleet and killing more than 2,000 American servicemen. The World War had begun.

THE WORLD AT WAR

The United States and Japan
The irony of the assault on Pearl Harbour was that it had been predicted. As early as January, 1941, the American ambassador in Tokyo informed Washington that "the Japanese forces planned, in the event of trouble with the United States, to attempt a surprise mass attack on Pearl Harbour using all their military facilities." American Navy chiefs discounted this information, arguing that Japan lacked the capacity for such an attack.

In fact a confrontation between the United States and Japan was inherent in the rapid expansion of the latter power. Japan's siezure of Manchuria, and her full-scale invasion of China in 1936, shocked American public opinion, and also threatened United States' interests in the area. Japan's booming economy needed new outlets, new sources of raw materials, new client states. Japanese policy-makers hoped to build a Greater East Asia Co-Prosperity sphere. This led to Japan moving into French Indo-China when France fell in 1940. The Dutch East Indies were also tempting prospective conquests, chiefly because of their oil deposits that the Japanese war machine so desperately needed.

Some of President Roosevelt's advisers pressed for a firm stand against Japan's rising ambitions, but their views did not at first prevail. Only in November 1941 did Japan make a series of diplomatic demands that amounted to an ultimatum. The United States reiterated its objection to Japanese expansion on the Asian mainland. The Japanese government, with its strong militarist composition, now felt that war was unavoidable.

Japan's strategy was fairly straightforward. She would quickly seize the oilfields of the Dutch East Indies. Singapore would be occupied, and so would the Philippines. The United States' Pacific fleet would have to be knocked out to prevent it disrupting these plans. Japanese power would then be extended to the borders of India in the west, to New Guinea in the south, and to the Gilbert Islands in the east. With Europe distracted by war, and with the American homeland apparently free from Japanese attacks, Japan calculated that she could defend her new conquests until they were accepted as permanent additions to her empire (C.21).

The raid on Pearl Harbour was thus an integral part of this strategy. Indeed Roosevelt let it be known that he would not "be surprised over a Japanese surprise attack." Nonetheless, the American defenders of Pearl Harbour *were* surprised by the waves of Japanese bombers that began to swoop from the skies at 7.55 a.m. on 7th December. Yet an American sailor had seen about twenty-five aircraft circling at 7.30, but had not identified them as Japanese. American radar was not yet a particularly sophisticated instrument, but it picked up the blips of the approaching host of torpedo and dive bombers. The radar scanners, however, chose to interpret this as evidence that American bombers were approaching from the mainland.

At 9.45 a.m. the aircraft withdrew. They left a scene of appalling devastation behind them. Three battleships were sunk and sixteen warships damaged – some of them seriously. Two thirds of the naval aircraft were destroyed, and only sixteen American bombers were left operational. As the stunned defenders of Pearl Harbour recovered, they managed to fight back, and in all twenty-nine Japanese planes were shot down. Although Japan seemed to have scored an enormous strategic triumph (the only justification for the attack), events were to prove otherwise. The tide of Japanese conquest in the Pacific and south-east Asia would not, in all probability, have been checked immediately by the American Pacific fleet. Moreover, as the Pacific war unfolded, aircraft carriers emerged as the key to victory. Yet the two American carriers in the Pacific fleet were not even in Pearl Harbour during the fateful attack.

From a political point of view, Japan's bombing of Pearl Harbour was a catastrophic blunder. President Roosevelt denounced the day of the raid as one that "would live in infamy" (2.27). American neutrality was finally cast aside, and Hitler helped to seal his own doom by declaring war on the United States. From now onwards "the arsenal of democracy", as Churchill had described the American Republic, would bring its enormous industrial potential to the aid of embattled Britain and Russia (4.10). The loss of the Pacific fleet at Pearl Harbour was to win the war for the allies.

Japan Triumphant (1941-2)

Japan followed up Pearl Harbour with a massive assault on British, Dutch and American territory throughout the Pacific. Within three days of 7th December, the Japanese had destroyed forty-two American aircraft on the ground in the Philippines, and had sunk the battleships H.M.S. *Prince of Wales*, and H.M.S. *Repulse*, thus destroying Britain's only two ships in eastern waters. On Christmas Day, 1941, Hong Kong surrendered and on 15th February, 1942, the great British imperial bastion of Singapore came crashing down leaving well over 100,000 Commonwealth troops as prisoners.

In February an allied fleet was almost totally eliminated in the Java Sea, and shortly afterwards the British naval presence in the Indian Ocean was effectively wiped out. In May the British evacuated Burma, by which time the whole of the Dutch East Indies and the Philippines had fallen to Japan, and Australia seemed in peril (5.11).

But even as the rising sun appeared to have reached its zenith there were signs that Japan faced the prospect of ultimate defeat. First there was the naval battle of the Coral Sea in May, 1942. The Japanese lost more aircraft than the Americans and had all their carriers immobilised. The failure to destroy the American carriers in the first days of the Pacific war was now weighing heavily upon Japan.

At first this was not apparent to the Japanese high command. Admiral Yamamoto believed, mistakenly, that two American carriers had been sunk in the battle of the Coral Sea. In general Japan's naval, and even military, efforts continued to be dissipated over wide areas. Perhaps early success had led to over-confidence. At any rate the turning point in the Pacific war came with the battle of Midway. By timing his aircraft strike to coincide with the refuelling of the Japanese carrier-based planes, Rear-Admiral Spruance knocked out Admiral Yamamoto's Air Arm by sinking four aircraft carriers. In five minutes, the balance of the war in the Pacific had been altered, and Japan, having lost the initiative, had to face the increasingly successful counter-attacks of her enemies.

The Turning of the Tide (1942-4)

Despite the dramatic conquests made by the Axis powers, by the early months of 1942, the odds against their long term success were shortening rapidly. The British Empire, the Soviet Union and the United States made a mighty confederacy, which was for the moment acting together against the common foe. A host of allied nations, many of them represented by governments in exile, supported the three giants. From General de Gaulle's Free French movement to the dispossessed leaders of smaller prostrate peoples, there was a desire to regain lost lands (C.31).

An allied invasion of Europe, however, was not on the cards in 1942. Soviet Russia called, understandably, for a Second Front in the west. The cry was taken up by left-wing sympathisers in Britain (4.5). From a military point of view this agitation was unpopular, and the disastrous Dieppe Raid of August, 1942, seemed to confirm that the military planners were right. More satisfying were the activities of British Bomber Command. In May the R.A.F. launched a thousand bomber raid on Cologne. Other German cities, some of them of great historical interest, were attacked (5.25). This was good for British morale, but the 1942 bombing offensive inflicted only slight damage on the German war economy.

In the Mediterranean and North Africa events favoured the allies by the end of 1942. Although Malta remained a battered citadel of British strength, and although Rommel broke through to within sixty miles of Alexandria by July, November brought welcome relief. At El Alamein, the new commander of the Eighth Army, Sir Bernard Montgomery, attacked Rommel's positions. On 4th November, the Axis troops began to retreat. British losses had been heavy, but there had been no mock heroics about the victory. Montgomery had managed to inspire his troops with confidence, and had also prudently waited until he possessed a marked superiority in tanks and artillery. He had then hit hard at Rommel's point of greatest strength. As church bells in Britain were rung to celebrate the victory, the Eighth Army began its pursuit of the Axis armies.

Three days after Montgomery broke Rommel at El Alamein, an Anglo-American invasion force landed in French North Africa. Progress was slow at first. The Germans fought stubbornly even when defeat seemed certain. In May, 1943, the Anglo-American forces under General Dwight Eisenhower linked up with Montgomery's armies coming from the east. On 12th May Axis resistance in North Africa ceased. Three quarters of a million prisoners were taken by the victors. The Mediterranean became safer for allied shipping and the pressure was taken off Malta.

There was, of course, still a long way to go to final victory. France had not been invaded, and Stalin still pressed in vain for a Second Front. In the meantime the eastern front was looking much healthier (C.9). At the end of 1942 Soviet forces destroyed a large German army at the battle of Stalingrad. Although a year would pass before the Germans were pushed away from

Leningrad in the north, the initiative had clearly passed to Russia. In addition, the Red Army was now able to boast superior numbers and a marked superiority in tanks, self-propelled guns, and fighter aircraft. The march on Berlin was beginning (2.46).

The summer of 1943 also saw the allies decisively winning the Battle of the Atlantic. The sinking of U-boats increased substantially, while merchant shipping losses dropped (5.18). Much of the credit for this change went to the American navy which was now providing hundreds of escort ships for the transatlantic convoys. The R.A.F. hit U-boats bases hard, while the Royal Navy knocked out Hitler's last battleship the *Tirpitz*, and sank the battle-cruiser *Scharnhorst*. Meanwhile Bomber Command and the U.S.A.F. continued to pound Germany. Far from crippling the German economy the raids probably stiffened German civilians' determination to make good the damage inflicted by the bombs. Germany's war production suffered at most a 9 per cent loss.

In July, 1943, Allied forces, having conquered North Africa, invaded Sicily. Within three weeks Mussolini was toppled from the leadership of his nation, and a new government made friendly overtures to the Allies. Under some pressure from Britain the Americans agreed to invade Italy, but in return they forced Churchill to press on with plans for the invasion of France—"Operation Overlord." Churchill preferred the attack on Italy, the "soft under belly" of the Axis powers, to the complexity and cost of an invasion of France. Perhaps he hoped for a quick victory on the cheap before Britain's great power status declined still further *vis-à-vis* the Soviet Russia and the United States.

The Allied attack on Italy, however, proved hazardous and expensive. Although the Italian government signed an armistice in September, 1943, their erstwhile German allies had already pushed troops far down the Italian peninsular. When Anglo-American forces fought their way ashore at Salerno, south of Naples, they found it impossible to make much headway in the drive north. By December, 1943, there was deadlock. The allies were held south of Rome along the Gustav line, and with Cassino, dominated by its ancient monastery, as a bulwark in the west.

In January, 1944, a landing was made at Anzio, which was to the north of the Gustav line. At first the plan seemed doomed to failure because the allied troops were hemmed in and reinforcements were unable to reach them. It was not until Cassino had been bombed into fragments in May 1944 that the general allied advance enabled the troops to make the breakout from Anzio. General Mark Clark entered Rome in triumph on 4th June. By December, 1944, the Allies had fought their way past Pisa, Florence and Ravenna, and the rest of Italy was quickly conquered after the great offensive of April, 1945. Mussolini was executed by Italian partisans, and his corpse, together with that of his mistress, ignominiously hanged by the heels for all to see.

D-Day and the Defeat of Germany (1944-5)

Two days after the American 7th Army took Rome, allied forces made a landing on the coast of Normandy. The D-Day operation, under the supreme command of General Eisenhower, began the last phase of the war in Europe. Hitherto, the Russians, at appalling human and material cost, had fought the Germans almost single-handed. Now the Second Front, for so long demanded by Stalin, became a reality. Even so, the fall of the Third Reich was not a foregone conclusion. The final Allied victory did not come for eleven months after D-day, and the German secret weapons, the V1 and the V2, began to fall on London after the Normandy landings.

Still, the planning behind D-day was impressive and thorough, and augured well for the success of the operation. The supreme commander, Eisenhower, though possessing little experience of active service, was diplomatic, and understood the priorities. His deputy was British–Air Marshal Tedder; both the air commander and the naval commander were also British. Montgomery was to direct the landings and then remain in command of the British army group. In all, three and a half million men were poised to invade France; American troops encamped in the south-west of England, British and Canadian forces in the south east. There were also 1,200 warships, 1,600 merchant ships, 4,000 assault craft, and over 13,000 aircraft.

Elaborate schemes had been devised to ensure the success of the operation. Most important perhaps was the attempt to convince the German high command that the main invasion was aimed at the Pas de Calais, not at Normandy. To aid this deception, fleets of dummy ships were assembled in south-eastern ports and intensive military activity was simulated in Kent and Sussex. The Germans were also misled by false information that was allowed to fall into their hands. In fact, when the Normandy landings took place, the majority of German troops were far away, east of the River Seine.

Allied scientists and technicians had developed two startlingly novel aids for the invasion. One was the Mulberry harbour, a prefabricated harbour that could be towed across the Channel and used to land essential supplies and reinforcements while ports like Cherbourg were being repaired. The other was PLUTO (pipe-line-under-the-ocean) by which the fuel so vital for modern mechanised warfare could be pumped from the Isle of Wight to Normandy. Neither of these technical masterstrokes were fully effective. One of the two Mulberry harbours was wrecked by violent storms shortly after D-day, while PLUTO only began functioning when Allied forces were liberating Belgium.

German defences along the French, Dutch and Belgian coasts were no great deterrent (10.6). The much vaunted Atlantic Wall was only nearing completion between Antwerp and Le Havre by D-day. Perhaps its chief value was as a morale-booster for the German divisions who would have to defend it. Of the two distinguished German generals committed to the defence of Hitler's western conquests, Von Rundstedt (the Commander-in-

Chief in the West) believed that an Allied landing could not be prevented, while Rommel (commanding the armies defending the coast from the Zuider Zee to the Loire) argued that if the invasion could not be crushed on the beaches in the first twenty-four hours then a breakout could not be prevented.

On 5th June, 1944, Eisenhower was promised a break in the stormy weather that had affected the Channel; he launched the greatest amphibious operation in history with the phlegmatic words, "O.K. Let's go." On 6th June the invasion force hit the Normandy beaches. Although American troops on the Omaha sector were bloodied, the first phase of the operation was a brilliant success. Confused by the jamming of their radar installations, their *Luftwaffe* harried by long-range American fighters, and with Allied naval supremacy unchallenged, the Germans reeled back along a thirty mile stretch of the Atlantic Wall. On 6th June 156,000 Allied troops were put ashore at the cost of 2,500 dead (mostly on the Omaha sector).

Despite the success of the D-day landings, it took some time for the Allies to capture Caen and to breakout into the French hinterland. Finally on 25th July the Americans broke through in the west. Von Rundstedt's dramatic counter-offensive eventually petered out. Paris was liberated on 25th August, and General De Gaulle made haste to assert his authority. By winter, however, the Rhine had not been reached, Germany was not defeated. In February, 1945, R.A.F. Bomber Command was allowed to obliterate the ancient town of Dresden causing up to 250,000 deaths.

But by March, 1945, the end of the war in Europe was in sight. The victorious Soviet armies controlled most of Eastern Europe and were making rapid headway against crumbling German resistance (C.36). On 7th March the Americans crossed the Rhine, and two weeks later Montgomery's armies also crossed further north. The triumphant forces of the Grand Alliance converged on the remnants of the Reich that was to have endured for a thousand years (C.12).

As the Anglo-American armies plunged deeper into Germany they uncovered the true horror of Nazi tyranny, just as the Russians had already done in eastern Europe. The troops that rode with the tanks into the vile stench of the concentration and extermination camps were presented with gross evidence of the unspeakable cruelties of the Nazi regime. Hitler, the architect of these abominations, was trapped in his Berlin bunker. On 30th April, with the Russians in the outskirts of Berlin, he committed suicide, having previously married his mistress Eva Braun. On 4th May the German armies opposing Montgomery in the north-west surrendered unconditionally. On 7th May the Germans surrendered on all fronts unconditionally.

Victory in Europe brought almost as many problems as the war itself. Millions had seen their homes destroyed, or had been uprooted from their traditional environments. In the territories overrun by the Red Army, the Russians actively encouraged communist takeover. British and American hostility to this perhaps inevitable development was of no avail. Perhaps

Stalin, having seen his country suffer indescribable devastation, was justifiably intent on guaranteeing his western frontiers. At any rate, while the Yalta Conference early in 1945 had seen a good deal of Allied accord over the future of the liberated territories, the Potsdam Conference at the end of July saw the first icy premonitions of the Cold War.

Of the three great powers only the United States could be said to have profited completely from the war. Great Britain faced serious economic difficulties, and soon the unprecedented growth of nationalist pressures within the Empire. Churchill had behaved throughout the war as the leader of a world power, but by 1945 the leadership of the non-communist world was the United States, for the asking. Britain was massively in debt, chiefly to the United States. Her export trade was a mere 40 per cent of the pre war total. As heroic an effort would be needed to win the post war production battle as had been called for in the aftermath of Dunkirk (4.3).

The Soviet Union had also suffered terrible losses. Perhaps 20 million Russians were killed during the Second War, most of them civilians. Cities, towns and villages were devastated. Huge areas of industry and agriculture had been badly dislocated. But despite all this, Russia emerged from the war against Hitler assured of great power status. The systematic transfer of industry over the Urals opened up her areas for development. The Soviet war machine was well-supplied and efficient (4.8). Technology had been given a powerful boost by the needs of war. The western frontiers were now secure.

In the rest of Europe, three major powers had each been defeated, though in different ways. Germany had been heavily and consistently bombed; the armies of invasion (particularly the Russians) had also wreaked havoc. Nearly four and a quarter million Germans lost their lives in the war, a fraction of Russia's losses and less even than Poland's but a large total nonetheless. Germany's loss of great power status was, in a way, more significant. The Fatherland was stripped of all the appurtenances of independent nationhood, and the Allied powers established zones of occupation. The Nazi leadership was put on trial at Nuremberg. Hitler, Goebbels and Himmler had previously committed suicide; Goering did so while in his death cell. In all twenty-one of the Nazi hierarchy were tried at Nuremberg, eleven of whom were hanged. Subsequently, hundreds more were brought to justice. As Fritzche, one of the accused, was to remark, "No power on heaven or on earth can take this shame away from my country."

Germany's ally Italy had also suffered invasion and much heavy fighting, but had changed sides in time. No Italian leaders were brought to trial after Mussolini's execution. Generally speaking, Italian post war recovery was encouraged by the Allies. France, of course, was one of the victorious powers, and was allotted a zone of occupation in Germany. Yet the victory had been won chiefly through the efforts of other nations, more resolute in their opposition to the Nazis. For the foreseeable future France had lost credibility as a great power.

Victory over Japan

Victory in Europe did not bring universal peace. In the Pacific and south-east Asia, the Allies were still relentlessly pushing Japanese forces out of the occupied territories. In Burma a hard slog by the Anglo-Indian army took them into Rangoon on 4th May, 1945. The United States was conducting the Pacific war with panache and determination, driving the Japanese from their island conquests, and eventually bombing the Japanese mainland. But Japan was by no means beaten by the summer of 1945. The troops of the Imperial Japanese army fought with determination and resilience, the Japanese economy still functioned efficiently.

It was in these circumstances that the Americans decided to bring the war to an abrupt end by dropping atomic bombs on Japan. This new and horrifying weapon had been developed by British and American scientists. President Truman, who had succeeded Roosevelt as President in April 1945, decided that the bombs should be used. Britain gave her consent; it is difficult to see what else she could have done. On 6th August, Hiroshima was obliterated, and on 9th August this the same fate overtook Nagasaki. Five days later the Japanese government decided to surrender.

The Second World War had come to an end. But it had ended in a way which confronted the post war world with profound moral problems. The cataclysmic energies released over Hiroshima and Nagasaki boded ill for mankind's future, just as the appalling after effects of radiation shocked opinion throughout the world. It was hoped that the United Nations Organisation, formed as the war was drawing to its close, would provide a suitable framework for reconciling international rivalries. It was all the more urgent to achieve such understanding now that the two new super powers, the United States and the Soviet Union, slipped further and further into mutual mistrust and hostility. The Second World War had provided mankind with an abundance of lessons – military, economic, political, social and moral. Whether any real notice would be taken of these lessons was still uncertain in 1945.

THE WAR AND THE PEOPLE

The war affected the daily lives of more people than any other conflict in history had done before. To begin with, more than 37,500,000 people lost their lives as a result of the war. Perhaps 20,000,000 of these were Russians. Both Poland and Germany each lost over 4,000,000. In addition, probably 6,000,000 Jews perished. Thus, through death, the war reached into every corner of the countries involved.

But not only lives were lost. The Blitz, the invasions of France and the Low Countries, the Russian campaign, the Pacific War, and finally the devastating assault on Nazi Germany, all these account for the ruin of countless homes and buildings. In the Soviet Union some 1,700 towns and cities had been destroyed – among them Kiev, Smolensk, Stalingrad and Minsk. Allied bombing had reduced the industrial heartland of the Ruhr to rubble. In Poland 21·5 per cent of pre war dwellings had been destroyed, in France 7·6 per cent, and even Norway lost 3·6 per cent.

More than this, for millions of people the war meant the destruction of the very society in which they lived. Central and Eastern Europe were particularly affected. Russia had taken over the Baltic states in 1940, and both Poland and Germany had their frontiers drastically reshaped at the peace. From the Soviet border to East Germany, communist governments were set up. Germany was beaten into unconditional surrender and put under military rule.

Even where frontiers remained intact, many nations suffered from the uprooting of huge numbers of the civilian population. Six million Jews had been exterminated, most of them coming from Poland and occupied Russia. Millions of non-Jews sought new homelands. These "displaced persons" were often sheltered in camps until room could be found for them in a restructured Europe. Of the great powers involved in the war only the United States escaped substantial material destruction on its home front. Britain also managed to maintain her political institutions and the overall framework of her society free from interference.

The Home Fronts

BRITAIN The opening months of the war were calm enough. Though there had been a widespread belief that earlier horrendous prophecies of great airial attacks would be immediately fulfilled, the Blitz did not begin in earnest until a year after the declaration of war. Nonetheless shelters were built, sandbags piled up, and gas masks issued (5.20). The shelters were not needed for a while; the gas masks fortunately were never needed. After the first great flood of evacuees to the countryside, there was a steady drift back to the towns. Although places of public entertainment closed for a while, they soon reopened.

The Blitz changed much of this. Above all it altered the pattern of life for millions of towndwellers. London in particular, bombed for seventy-six nights in succession, was drastically affected (1.11). Thousands chose to sleep on the platforms of Underground stations, a habit which persisted even after the Blitz had died away. For countless others on the surface the night's sleep was broken by the thump of falling bombs or by the noise of anti-aircraft fire from the ground. The light of morning would often reveal an altered townscape: an office block burned down here, a group of terraced houses shattered there.

British losses from bombing raids were markedly less than those suffered by Germany – about 60,000 as opposed to over half a million. Nonetheless the Blitz, chiefly through its destruction of housing, caused a heavy uprooting of the civilian population. The second evacuation which attended the Blitz was also significant in giving towndwellers an insight into country life, and, more important, in showing country people that the children of the urban poor were still grossly underprivileged. The crossing of class and environmental frontiers in the Blitz stimulated a general feeling that social reforms were needed.

The communal perils of the Blitz, and the aftermath of Dunkirk, helped to foster a national community sense (C.27). In the factories absenteeism and industrial disputes declined sharply (4.3). Men were prepared to give up holidays and work longer hours. The rationing of food and clothing also had their effect. The wealthy could still dine handsomely at famous restaurants, but most people had to subsist on portions of food that would have been considered downright inadequate in pre war days (6.6). But the wartime cafeterias supplied plain cheap and nutritious meals, and the Ministry of Food offered recipes, sometimes consisting of bizarre ingredients, to make the most of existing supplies (C.26).

Clothes rationing was another levelling factor. Many families made good use of old clothes; for others the range of new clothes was tightly restricted, and exotic colours became hard to find. But while the people had to be clothed and fed as best as possible, it was also essential to meet their other needs with the utmost efficiency and fairness. For example, air raid casualties were given free medical treatment; and vitamins, cod-liver oil, and orange juice were made available to ensure public health.

The production battle was as vital as the military battle, and the government tried to keep men and women satisfied in their work (4.4). Under the influence of J. M. Keynes, the Treasury called for full employment. The Beveridge Plan, published in 1942, outlined the future Welfare State. More immediately, the average weekly wage rose by 80 per cent during the war, while the cost of living rose by only 31 per cent. Subsequently workers were better off under the wartime economy than they had been in peacetime. Government food subsidies helped to maintain this happy state of affairs.

Since so many people were actively involved in the war effort, had endured so many hardships, and made so many sacrifices, the end of the war in Europe saw the people in a mood for change. The General Election of 1945 returned Labour with a crushing majority over the Conservatives. Grateful to Churchill for his conduct of the war, the electorate preferred to put their trust in Labour for the peace. Once in power Clement Attlee's government pushed through a heavy programme of nationalisation and social reform. Their task was doubtless made easier both by Labour's participation in Churchill's Wartime Coalition; and by the achievements of "wartime socialism". Often the new government did little more than put into statute form the effects of the greater centralisation that had been needed to win the war. Thus the "social revolution" of 1945-51 had its roots firmly in the years of the Second World War.

GERMANY AND OCCUPIED EUROPE Even among the Nazi hierarchy few could have predicted the extent of Germany's early successes in the war. The easy conquest of Poland, Denmark, Norway, Belgium, the Netherlands and finally France, immeasurably strengthened Hitler's hold over his people. The propaganda minister Joseph Goebbels capitalised on the military breakthrough. Posters, newsreels, and broadcasts glorified the triumphant campaigns of *Wermacht* and *Luftwaffe* (2.16). The result of the Battle of Britain was concealed from the majority of the nation.

The German people were adequately fed for the first half of the war, due to food rationing and the availability of food from conquered countries. The bombing raids of the R.A.F. did not inflict heavy damage or large-scale loss of life until after 1941. In 1942, indeed, the government considered that there was no need as yet to divert more of the economy to the production of armaments.

Although the army had triumphed so spectacularly up to December, 1941, the traditional political influence of the German generals had been deliberately eroded. In occupied areas the *Gauleiters* (all party men) were put in charge of the administration. In cases of civil emergency, these men, who were directly responsible to Hitler, would make the vital decisions. The growth of the *Waffen-S.S.* was another example of the Nazis' determination to make use of alternatives to the army (1.4). The S.S., some 600,000 by 1945, was the force which carried out the mass deportations and mass executions. Together with the Gestapo it provided the essential support for the system of concentration camps, extermination camps and police terror.

At the outbreak of war many new laws were passed setting the death penalty on a wide variety of offences. The numbers of those condemned to death rose precipitately. As the war progressed, thousands of those politically suspect were sent to the concentration camps. Earlier, from 1939-41, some 70,000 of Germany's mentally ill had been killed in accordance with Hitler's secret order of September, 1939.

But it was the Nazis' treatment of the Jews that was the most horrific part of the activities of a brutal regime (C.24). Contempt and distrust of the Jews was fundamental to Hitler's avowed desire to exclude them from a respectable place in German society (8.2). After the Nazis' accession to power, Jewish people within the Reich were systematically and humiliatingly subordinated. Eventually they were forbidden, among other things, to use public telephones, to own pets, or typewriters or spectacles. Before the outbreak of war a great many German and Austrian Jews had left their homelands for safer refuge.

The German conquest of Poland, Eastern Europe and the Ukraine, however, brought seven million Jews under Nazi rule. In Denmark and Norway the small Jewish communities were afforded a certain amount of protection and thus left more or less intact, but in Vichy France Jews were made the objects of legal discrimination. When Hitler invaded Russia, the treatment of Jews took a new and ominous turn. Probably before the invasion Hitler gave verbal orders for the extermination of Jews in occupied territories. In January, 1942, Heinrich Heydrich, charged by Goering to destroy the Jewish influence in Europe, spoke of the "final solution to the Jewish problem".

The final solution entailed on-the-spot mass executions, the systematic deportation of Jews to concentration camps, and the establishment of ghettos. During the first five months of the Russian campaign special detachments executed some 400,000 Jewish people per month. Eventually nearly one and a half million Jews were obliterated in Russia, many of them simply machine-gunned down. In Poland, Jews from the Warsaw ghetto were either starved to death or transported to the extermination camp at Treblinka.

A network of death camps was established. The most infamous was at Auschwitz in Upper Silesia where the killing of the inmates was approached in an inhumanly efficient manner. The most common means of extermination was to herd thousands of Jews into large gas chambers and then poison them with Prussic acid. Those who died in the gas chambers were relatively fortunate compared with those who were worked to death or made the objects of sadistic medical experiments.

Under Himmler, the Reichsfuhrer S.S., and Adolf Eichmann, who was responsible for Jew-hunting and deportation, a huge bureaucratic-industrial system carried out the "final solution". Ironically the transport facilities claimed by the S.S. took vitally-needed vehicles away from the German Army in its long retreat from the Eastern front. Hitler ordered an end to the extermination programme in 1944, but the killings continued. It is inconceivable that the German nation knew nothing of these activities. But equally the Allies seem to have done little to save those Jews who might possibly have escaped. The Jews were transported to the death camps without a struggle, and, once there, often voluntarily entered the gas chambers under the impression that they were merely shower rooms. Even a nation so used to persecution could not appreciate the full horror and inevitability of the final solution.

A large number of people in the occupied countries were put to work by Germany. By 1945 more than 8,000,000 foreigners were working in Germany, and nearly 30 per cent of industrial workers were non-Germans. The status of these foreign workers differed dramatically. At the top of the scale were the French and Belgians who had come voluntarily to the Third Reich in pursuit of higher wages—some simply in pursuit of work of any kind (10.1). At the bottom of the scale were the Russians and Poles, the "sub-humans" of Nazi racial theories. Russian workers wore badges bearing one word *Ost* (East); it was a sufficient description.

Hitler had initially wanted to keep Russian prisoners out of Germany, but by 1942 the desperate needs of German industry forced a change in policy.

C.1 *American*
(David Store
Martin)
A mixture of
crusading,
religious and
industrial
symbolism.

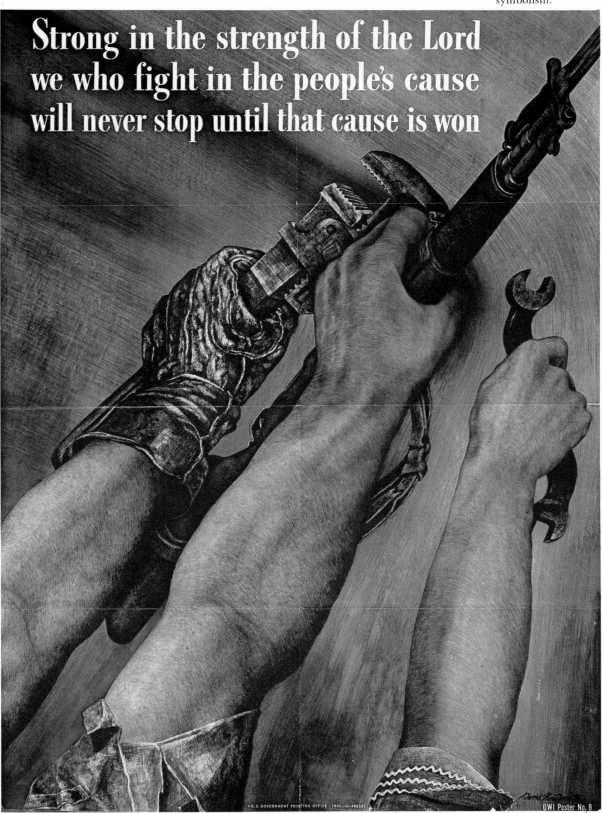

Strong in the strength of the Lord
we who fight in the people's cause
will never stop until that cause is won

C.4 *Belgian* (opposite)
"Everything is going very well . . .
Madame la Marquise". A
collaborationist poster, based on a
popular French song.

C.2 *British*
A poster based on a Russian
original presented to Lord
Beaverbrook by Stalin.

C.3 *British*
A powerful image.

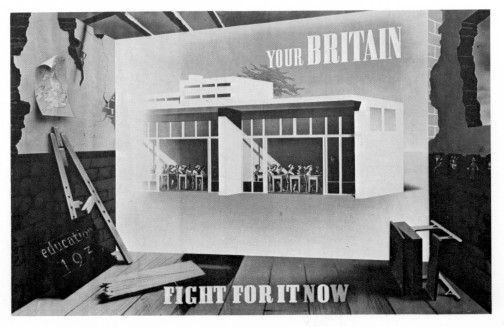

C.5 *Belgian*
"Entente Cordiale"
A mocking interpretation of the
Grand Alliance by
collaborationists.

C.6 *British*
One of the "banned posters" of
World War Two. The A.T.S. girl
was considered too glamorous for
the serious business of war
recruitment.

Work on a farm...
this Summer

JOIN THE U.S. CROP CORPS
SEE YOUR U.S. EMPLOYMENT SERVICE OR YOUR LOCAL COUNTY AGENT

ГИТЛЕРИАДА
/ КРАТКАЯ БИОГРАФИЯ ФАШИСТСКОГО ГАДА /.

В ФАШИСТСКОМ ВОЗРАСТЕ СВОЕМ ЕЩЕ ЗЕЛЕНОМ
У ФАБРИКАНТОВ ОН НАЕМНЫМ БЫЛ ШПИОНОМ:
СТАРАЯСЬ ИЗ ПОСЛЕДНИХ СИЛ,
ОН НА РАБОЧИХ ДОНОСИЛ.

ОРАТЕЛЬ ЯРОСТНО — ПОГРОМНЫЙ,
С ХОЗЯЕВ НЕ СПУСКАЯ ГЛАЗ,
ПО МЮНХЕНСКИМ ПИВНЫМ СБРОД ВЕРБОВАЛ ОН ТЕМНЫЙ,
ЧТОБ РАЗГРОМИТЬ РАБОЧИЙ КЛАСС.

ПАЛАЧ, ДИКАРЬ, „ВАЛЕТ" БАНКИРСКОЙ ЗЛОЙ ИГРЫ,
РАСИСТСКОЕ ПРИВИВ ГЕРМАНЦАМ ГНИЛОКРОВЬЕ,
ТВОРЕНЬЯ ГЕНИЕВ ОН СТАЛ ШВЫРЯТЬ В КОСТРЫ,
ЧТОБ ВОЗРОДИТЬ СРЕДНЕВЕКОВЬЕ.

„МЕЙН КАМПФ"! „МОЯ БОРЬБА"! КНИЖОНОЧКУ СВОЮ,
ФАШИСТСКУЮ ГАЛИМАТЬЮ
С „ИДЕОЛОГИЕЙ" РАЗБОЙНОЙ,
ОН ПРЕВРАТИЛ В СВОЮ ДОХОДНУЮ СТАТЬЮ:
ОНА ЯВЛЯЕТСЯ ЕГО КОРОВОЙ ДОЙНОЙ.

ЗВЕРЬ, „ГИТЛЕР—ЛЮДОЕД"— ОН МИР ПОТРЯС ВОЙНОЙ.
ФАШИСТСКИМ СДЕЛАТЬ ОН ХОТЕЛ ВЕСЬ ШАР ЗЕМНОЙ,
ПСОМ БЕШЕНЫМ НА ВСЕХ КИДАЯСЬ БЕЗ РАЗБОРА,
ОН В СХВАТКУ РИНУЛСЯ С СОВЕТСКОЮ СТРАНОЙ.
БАНДИТ ИЗВЕДАЛ МОЩЬ СОВЕТСКОГО ОТПОРА!

ЕЩЕ ОПАСЕН ЗВЕРЬ, ХОТЬ МЕЧЕТСЯ В БРЕДУ,
ВОСТОЧНЫЙ ФРОНТ, ХРИПЯ, ОН НАЗЫВАЕТ АДОМ
А ЗАПАД НОВУЮ ЕМУ СУЛИТ БЕДУ.
ТОВАРИЩИ, ВПЕРЕД! В СОРОК ВТОРОМ ГОДУ
ДОЛЖНЫ ПОКОНЧИТЬ МЫ С ФАШИСТСКИМ ПОДЛЫМ ГАДОМ!

ХУДОЖНИКИ - КУКРЫНИКСЫ   ТЕКСТ - Д. БЕДНЫЙ.

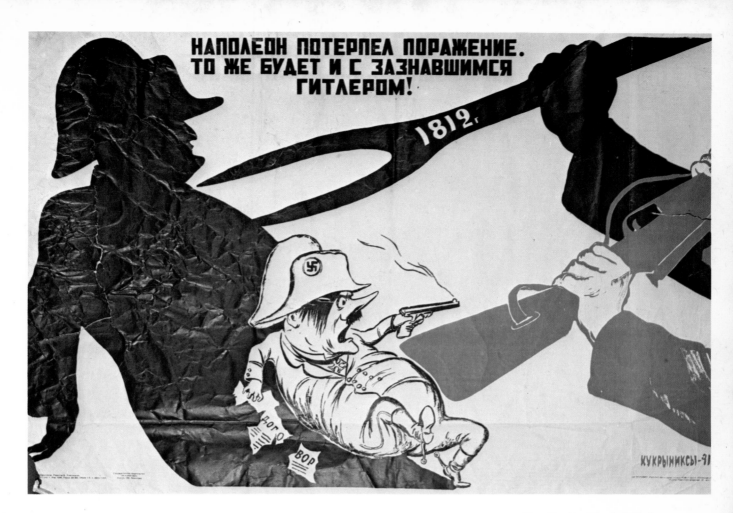

С.9 *Russian* (Koukrinikci)
"Napoleon suffered defeat. The same thing will happen to the conceited Hitler".

С.8 *Russian*
"A short Biography of Fascist Evil" in a comic-strip idiom.

C.10 *American* (Norman Rockwell)

fuori i tedesch

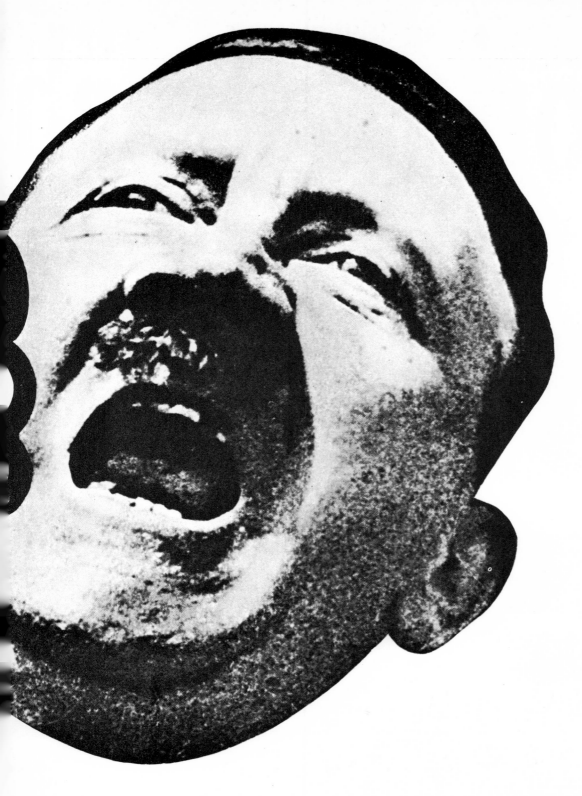

C.13 *Italian*
"Kick out the Germans".
A poster of the partisans.

ЕТРОВСК НАШ!

„С НОВЫМ ГОДОМ!"

НОВЫЙ ГОД!
С ФАШИСТСКОЙ СВОРОЙ
ПОЛНЫЙ БЛИЗИТСЯ РАСЧЁТ.
ЭТО БУДЕТ ГОД, В КОТОРОМ
ВРАГ КОСТЕЙ НЕ СОБЕРЕТ!

художник – П. Соколов-Скаля.   А. Жаров.

ФАКЕЛЬЩИК, БАНДИТ,
ОЛЯ ДАВ ТЯГУ,
ГУЮ ПЕРЕДРЯГУ.
РОВСК,—ПОДЛЕЦ ТВЕРДИТ,
МИИ НЕРОБКОЙ!—
ВЕСЬ КРЕДИТ,
ОТТУДА ПРОБКОЙ!

текст – ДЕМЬЯН-БЕДНЫЙ

C.14 *Russian*
"On tour from Germany–the
Hitler Circus!" Nazi leaders and
fascist statesmen cavort round
ringmaster Hitler in this lively
poster.

C.15 *Russian* (Lebedev)
"Duepropetrovsk is ours"
An action-packed poster
illustrating Russian military
success.

C.16 *Russian*
"Happy New
Year"
Sardonic and
revengeful.

We French workers w[ho know]
defeat means slavery

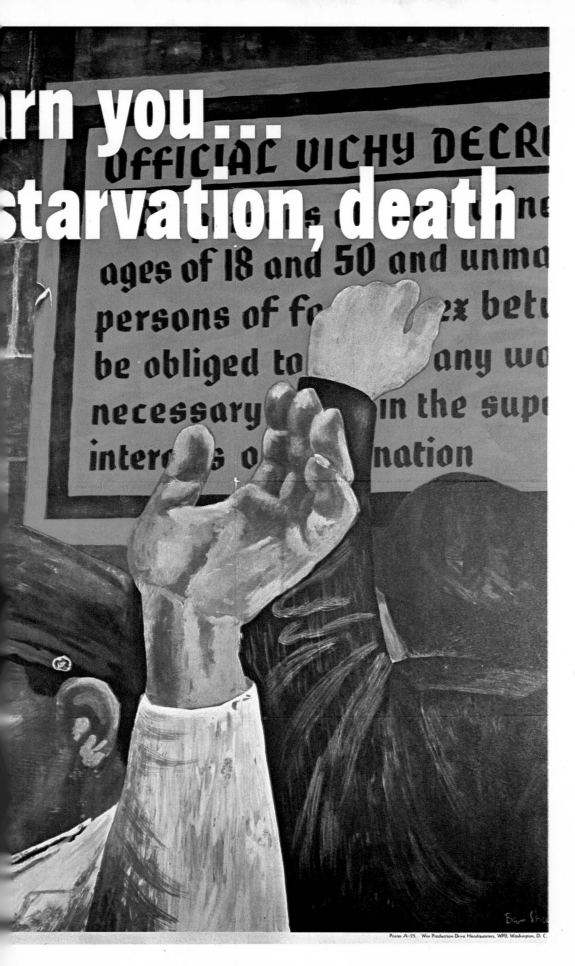

C.19 *German*
"Europe's Victory is Your Prosperity".
With Britain moribund, the mailed fist of Nazi Germany smashes Stalin and bolshevism.

C.18 *German* (Witte of Hamburg)
"Build Youth Hostels and Homes"
The central figure has the appeal of a Girl Guide.

Baut
Jugendherbergen
und Heime

Europas Sieg
dein Wohlstand

撃ちてし止まむ

第三十八回
陸軍記念日

陸軍省

C.21 *Japanese*

C.20 *Chinese* (Martha Sawyers)
Printed in the United States.
"United China Relief" was a U.S.
organization to help the Chinese
war effort.

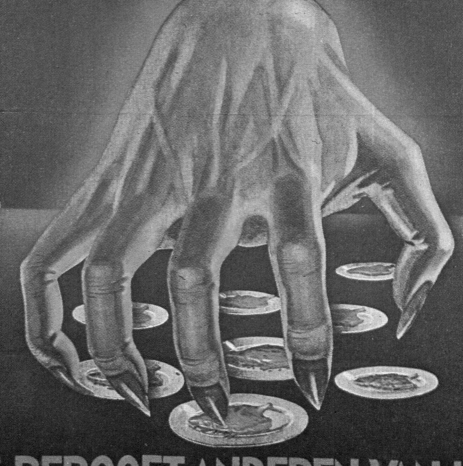

C.22 *Dutch* (opposite)
"Buying the meat of illegally slaughtered cattle is a crime."

C.23 *American* (1943)
The poster attacks the barbaric and anti-Christian nature of the Nazi movement. The dagger plunging into the Bible makes (no doubt consciously) the shape of a brutal cross, held by an arm decorated with the crooked Nazi cross.

C.24 *German*
"There is the cause of the War!" A simplistic exercise in vilification.

C.25 *American* (A. Parker)
American food production was
greatly increased during the war!

C.26 *British*
An attempt to sell hitherto
unpopular food.

C.27 *British* (Frank Newbould).

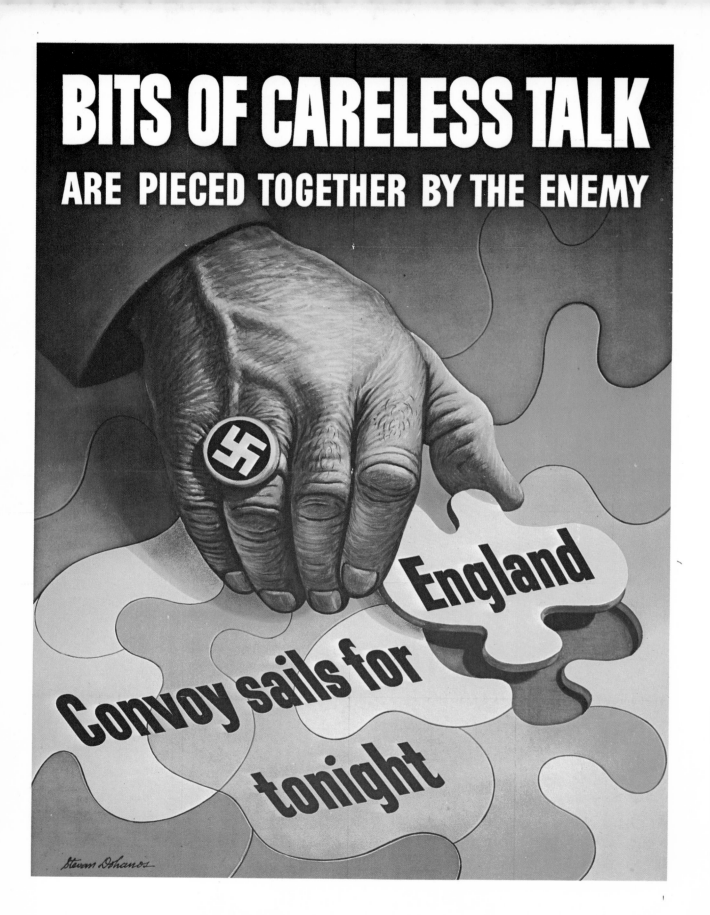

C.28 *American* (Stevan Dohanos).

ΟΙ ΗΡΩΙΔΕΣ ΤΟΥ 1940

C.29 *Greek*
"The heroines of 1940". A
tribute to the Greek resistance to
the Italian invasion of 1940.

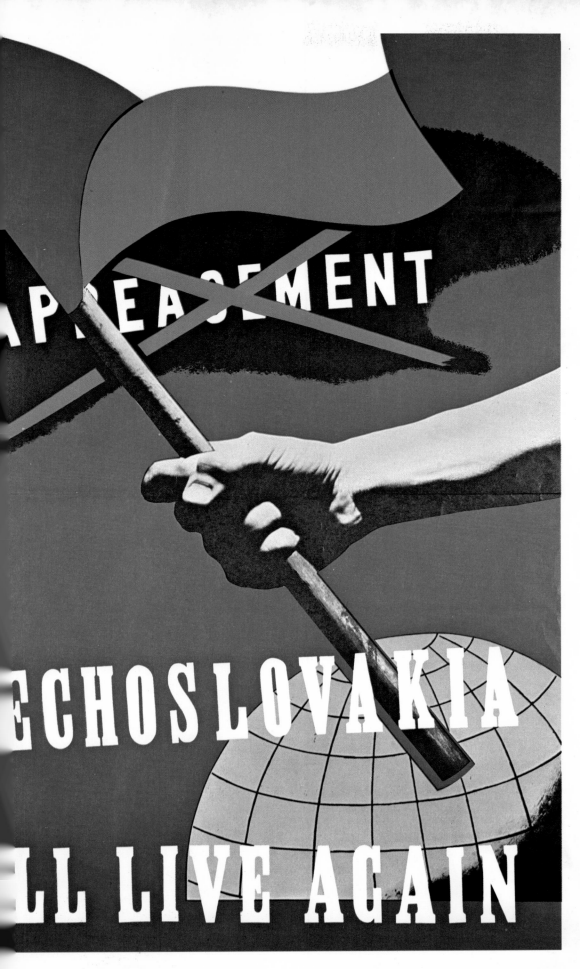

C.32 *American*
(Elmer)
Issued by the
"America First
Committee", a
body which aimed
to keep the U.S.A.
neutral.

C.33 *American* (Wesley)
(1943).

C.34 *Canadian*
(Everleigh).

C.35 *American* (opposite)
(Tom Woodburn).

WINGS OVER
AMERICA

AIR CORPS
U.S. ARMY

C.36 *Russian*
"Fight the German Beasts. It is
possible to destroy Hitler's army
and it is a duty"

Millions of Russians, both prisoners-of-war and civilians, were imported and set to work. The Russians were soon the largest group of foreign workers, and Russian women comprised over half of female workers from outside Germany. Workers from the east suffered very bad working conditions and low living standards. Their camps were much inferior to those of workers from the West, their rations were poorer, their medical treatment scanty, their pay was heavily taxed at source. Generally the productivity of the foreign workers was low, and where possible they resorted to sabotage. But the vast numbers employed meant that for much of the war the Nazi regime was able to make more effective use of German citizens in industry.

The German people mostly bore the burden of war with phlegmatic determination. Mass bombings by the R.A.F. and the U.S.A.F., though inflicting terrible material damage, did not break civilian morale (5.25). The first euphoric years of the war presented no problems to the state's propaganda machine. But by 1943 the failures on the Russian front and in North Africa presaged the beginning of the end, and "national solidarity" and self-sacrifice was now the aim of Goebbels' propaganda instead of exultation (2.21).

After 1942 Hitler drastically reduced his public speeches and appearances. This withdrawal offered Goebbels wide scope for shaping public opinion. The German people, with the casualty lists lengthening, could no longer hope for total victory. Rather, the looming prospect of a Russian invasion caused the regime to exalt stubborn loyalty and the dubious merits of dying in the last ditch (2.33). Perhaps the resulting mixture of foreboding and resolution encouraged the nation to blatantly ignore the evident sufferings of the Jews, slave workers and political prisoners.

THE SOVIET UNION By December 1941 one-third of European Russia and two-thirds of her industrial strength had been captured by the Germans. Of the twenty million Russians that died in the war, the great majority were either civilians or prisoners-of-war (9.6). The Russian people were thus more affected by the war than the people of any other Allied nation. For this reason Soviet historians have, with justice, described the Russo-German war as "The Great Patriotic War".

The first German thrusts in the Ukraine did not, however, automatically inspire Russian patriotism. Many Soviet citizens welcomed the Germans as liberators who would release them from the grip of the party machine, and collaboration was widespread. A short period of contact with the triumphant forces of nazism did much to dispel this illusion. Huge numbers of Russian prisoners were interned in hastily constructed camps and left to die of starvation and disease. As the Germans advanced thousands of civilians were left foodless and homeless (2.43). The mass shootings of civilians and partisans were brutal and commonplace; often those to be massacred were first made to dig their own graves. This campaign of terror united the Russian people in their resolve to tear the heart out of nazism.

One result of the early German successes was that the Russians moved industrial plant and equipment on a mammoth scale. Working round the clock, technicians and industrial labourers dismantled factories and transported them across the Urals, often into Siberia, where they were then reassembled. Thousands of workers were drafted into the new industrial areas, and in the latter half of 1941 more than a million housewives, students and school-children entered industry. Compulsory overtime was introduced and holidays abolished.

Food supply was a critical problem. The great agricultural areas of the Ukraine and the western regions had been overrun, and farms were stripped of tractors, cars and horses to supply the German army. At the end of 1943 the number of men working on collective farms was less than a third of the total in June 1941. Women and children played a vital part in maintaining adequate food supplies. Food rationing had been imposed in Moscow and Leningrad shortly after the German invasion and later it was imposed on the whole country. Workers were allotted bread rations according to the work they did: in heavy industry they were allowed 800 grammes to 1·2 kilogrammes per day; engineering and technical staff received 500 grammes, and office workers 400–450 grammes.

As in Britain, Soviet citizens were encouraged to "Dig for Victory", and urban dwellers tended allotments and cultivated waste land. Even so the amount of food eaten by the average citizen fell by some 38 per cent. Clothes in particular, and consumer goods in general, became extremely difficult to obtain. A booming trade in second-hand clothes developed, and cigarettes were such a luxury that they were often passed from hand to hand—sometimes for a certain amount of money per puff. In the towns the stores had little to display, and medical services ran short of supplies.

The besieged cities of Moscow and Leningrad were reduced to dreary imitations of their prewar personalities due to damage and neglect. Clothes rationing forced a dull uniformity on people, and the standard winter outfit was head scarves, padded top coats, and hats with ear-flaps. Queues formed everywhere, as they did in Britain, but in Russia people tended to wait longer and the food rations, when they came, were even less varied than their British equivalents. The demands of the fighting forces and of industry stripped the cities of young able-bodied men. The women who were left played an heroic part in keeping urban services going, often undertaking heavy and arduous work and sometimes only receiving food in payment.

Leningrad suffered particularly from its 900 day siege. It has been estimated that nearly a million of its three million inhabitants died—many from malnutrition and hunger. Curfews were imposed in major Russian cities, and military patrols were on the look-out for German spies and infiltrators.

When the German armies began their retreat they still wrought havoc on large areas of Russia. As they pulled out, the Germans laid waste the land they were evacuating. Factories and bridges were blown up, mines were flooded, power stations destroyed. During the war the Soviet state endured massive losses of material and property, as well as life. Some 17,000 towns were partly or wholly destroyed, as well as 70,000 villages, 84,000 schools, 40,000 miles of railway track, and 31,000 factories.

During the German retreat, as during the years of occupation, the Russian partisans continued to fight their enemy. At first the partisans were mainly composed of those liable to suffer most from the German occupation – party members, Komsomol (Communist Youth) members, Red Army men cut off from their units, and intellectuals. If caught by the Germans these people (together with the Jews) were handed over to the S.S. and exterminated. Later, as the real nature of the German occupation became evident, and especially when the Red Army went over to the offensive, the partisan movement drew on other sections of the population. Perhaps, eventually, a million partisans (many of them women) operated behind the enemy's lines.

They did so often at terrible cost to themselves. If captured, the partisans could expect at best a summary execution. Thousands met this fate, while others suffered interrogation, torture, and a slow death at the hands of the Gestapo. Partisans were under no illusion as to the conditions they would generally have to endure. They had to contend with the ferocious winter of 1941/2 and hunger was to be expected, while medical attention if wounded was by no means guaranteed. It seems as if many of the villagers in the areas of partisan activity were unsympathetic to the partisan cause, and betrayed them if it seemed expedient to do so.

The Germans responded to the partisan resistance by committing the worst atrocities of the Russian campaign. Whole villages suspected of supplying partisans were wiped out; hostages were hanged, and the subsistence needs of the civilian population callously disregarded (C.30). Unhappily the successes of the partisans were viewed with suspicion by the Communist hierarchy and in recently liberated areas they were automatically given security checks. Many were drafted into the army, and some were sent to labour camps. Their determination and courage, however, had given invaluable support to the Red Army. They had helped to justify the Russian description of World War Two as the Great Patriotic War.

JAPAN The defeat of Japan cost that nation two and a half million dead. Living standards dropped severely as a result of the conflict and ten million Japanese were homeless by the end of the war. The old order had been discredited and a democratic government was introduced under Allied occupation.

The Japanese showed little opposition to the war. There are several reasons for this. Firstly, since 1937 Japanese armed forces had been fighting a full-scale war in China (C.20). The war against the United States, Britain and the Netherlands could be interpreted as merely an extension (though an extremely hazardous one) of the existing war (C.21). Next, the Japanese economy was already geared to war by 1941, and the government had assumed wide

27

arbitrary powers in the national interest.

In 1940 all the major political parties had been liquidated, and a one party system established. The trade unions had been completely emasculated, and in 1941 membership was well under one thousand. A well-organised propaganda campaign had instilled the virtues of super-patriotism and unquestioning nationalism. Moreover, the nationwide establishment of popularly supported local and neighbourhood associations, which dealt with a large number of civil problems and organisation, had the effect of cementing traditional loyalties and stifling criticism.

For almost a year after Pearl Harbour the war gave little cause for pessimism. Japanese forces had triumphed in south-east Asia and although the American victory at the Battle of Midway in 1942 was an uncomfortable indication of future reverses, the almost effortless extension of Japanese power up to that point encouraged patriots and potential waverers alike. The Great East Asia Co-Prosperity Sphere, which was an economic grouping dominated by Japan, had become a reality. In Burma and the East Indies enough of the local population were prepared to see the Japanese as liberators. What had once been the accepted superiority of the great European imperialist powers was no longer acceptable after they had been decisively defeated by the Japanese.

The government was thus able to claim extraordinary military successes, while also shielding the people from Allied propaganda. Even liberals and intellectuals seem to have either supported the war enthusiastically, or kept quiet. The zeal of the state police doubtless accounted for much of this passivity, but it also indicates that nationalism had a traditional hold over all classes of Japanese society surpassing that of other combatant countries (2.8).

Despite the Great East Asia Co-Prosperity Sphere, Japan was particularly vulnerable to attacks on her economy. This was especially true of her import trade. Before the war Japan's merchant marine was inadequate, and Allied sinkings (culminating in the loss of 4,120,000 tons in 1944) made the position intolerable. Since 20 per cent of Japan's rice was imported the losses had a dire effect on the people's diet.

In 1942 the average weight of newborn babies had decreased by eight ounces. Many adults suffered from persistent stomach and bowel upsets. It has been estimated that the average daily intake of calories in 1945 was 1,680 as compared with a prewar average of 2,265. Rationing, after 1941, did something to ensure a fair distribution of food, but the Japanese people had to make use of certain staples (like potatoes, soya beans, and brown rice) which many would have rejected before the war.

As elsewhere among belligerent nations, the black market flourished in Japan. Between December 1943 and the final defeat in August 1945, horrendous price rises occurred. Leather shoes and soap rose by 1,000 per cent; sugar by 1,030 per cent, and matches by 8,000 per cent. Sales of consumer goods slumped badly by over 30 per cent. Many small businesses were ruined.

Wages rose by something like 100 per cent, but still lagged behind prices. Agricultural producers, however, benefiting from government subsidies, tended to do better than industrial workers.

In contrast to the European and North American belligerents, Japan did not make special use of women as factory workers. Perhaps traditional prejudices counted for something in all this. Thus in 1944, when industry became short of manpower, the government chose to deploy students in the factories rather than women. Between two and a half and three million women did join the nation's labour force from 1940 to 1945, but this was a relatively small proportion of the total female population.

In one other respect Japan underwent a wartime experience different from that of other nations. This was when atomic bombs were dropped on Nagasaki and Hiroshima in August 1945. The appalling consequences of these attacks enabled the Emperor Hirohito to throw his weight behind the growing peace party and to end the war. The dropping of the atomic bombs was, in some ways, merely a confirmation of an inevitable slide towards defeat. The earlier devastating air-raids on Japanese cities had already caused dreadful material damage and loss of life (nearly 200,000 citizens of Tokyo were killed by a raid in March 1945). The mushroom clouds over Hiroshima and Nagasaki meant that hundreds of thousands of Japanese did not die in the last ditch in more orthodox military encounters. And, ironically, unconditional surrender was to prove the first step to democratic forms of government and a steeply rising standard of living. Victory would not necessarily have brought the Japanese people so much.

THE UNITED STATES The Second World War was the largest war in which the United States had ever fought. Although some four million men had been engaged in the Civil War of 1861-5, and four and three-quarter million had fought in the Great War, between 1941 and 1945 more than sixteen million Americans served in the armed forces. Of these 406,000 died, and a further 700,000 were wounded. For the first time in the country's history, the number of Americans killed in battle exceeded those who were killed by disease—due largely to medical innovations like penicillin, the use of blood plasma, and DDT in combating malaria (1.13).

The war affected the American people not only through the casualty lists. The stimulation of the economy led to a dramatic and welcome fall in the total of unemployed (from 5,500,000 in 1939 to 670,000 in 1944). Equally significant, the standard of living rose steadily throughout the war years. Nor was this improvement swept away in a post war slump. In a way the Second World War was a generally profitable conclusion of Roosevelt's New Deal, though an unexpected one. The national debt rose from some $20 billion to over $200 billion, yet the American economy became healthier.

The war production of the United States reached a phenomenal level in a relatively short time (4.11). In the interwar years the world had seen how America could make refrigerators and automobiles; it now saw the factories

29

turn out a torrent of war planes, tanks, weapons and material of war. Between 1941 and 1945, over 300,000 war planes and 124,0000 ships were built, as were millions of trucks and other vehicles (4.10). Both Britain and Russia, received essential war supplies from the United States' production lines. The "Arsenal of Democracy" also advanced huge loans to these co-belligerents, especially the British Empire. American gold reserves rocketed, increasing by some £1,422,000,000 by 1945, while Britain owed about £5,000,000 in gold in 1945 and France £335,000,000.

The United States also possessed the enormous advantage of almost complete economic self-sufficiency. The most serious shortage to be met in the early months of the war was that of natural rubber. Japan's conquests in Malaya and the Dutch East Indies denied America fresh supplies of this essential war material and the government had to ration rubber for non-war uses, using the country's stockpiles. It also rapidly developed the synthetic rubber industry which, by the end of the war, enabled the vast military machine to run smoothly.

The country was endowed with a peaceful labour force as well (4.9). The big trade union organisations pledged themselves against strikes for the duration of the war, and with some exceptions, notably in the coal and rail road industries, this pledge was maintained. Perhaps the dramatic fall in unemployment helped to create better relations between workers and employers but the War Labor Board, set up by President Roosevelt, helped with the problem of settling disputes, and of aligning wage increases with rising prices. The Board also found it wise to grant unions a large number of "fringe benefits", such as holidays with pay, more holidays, travel allowances, and bonuses. These measures established a pattern for postwar labour demands, but were also valid reforms.

The Roosevelt government also managed to control prices, as a vital part in the bid to curb inflation. The Supplementary Price Control Act was passed in October 1942 and gave the President a real chance of controlling prices. In 1943 and 1944 prices rose only very slightly overall. Rationing was also introduced in 1942, but compared with the British or the Russian, the American civilian suffered little deprivation. Fifteen essential commodities (like rubber, oil, and sugar) were rationed and civilian boards were set up to supervise rationing, but the restrictions they had to enforce were hardly draconian.

The government also encouraged home agricultural expansion. Agricultural prices were allowed to rise steadily, and the nation not only fed itself more than adequately but was able to send large quantities of food to its allies. Between 1940 and 1944 over 30,000,000 acres of hitherto uncultivated land were brought into production. Though this was to lead to problems of over-production after the war, it was a triumph for the war effort of 1941-5 (C.7).

In general, the American nation was remarkably united during the war

(C.1). Propaganda posters laid heavy and persistent emphasis on the flag as a symbol of unity and on the equal responsibilities of soldier and factory worker (4.7). Although there were substantial minorities of German and Italian descent there was no serious opposition to the war. Although there was a Japanese population in the Pacific states there was no active subversion, though the government took the precaution of placing 18,000 Japanese in relocation centres until the end of hostilities. These measures were not enforced against the Japanese in Hawaii, who remained conspicuously loyal to United States' interests.

Political differences were submerged under the need to promote the war effort. The American Communist Party had no trouble in actively supporting the war after the German attack on Soviet Russia. Republican leaders played the part of Uncle Sam's loyal opposition, and Governor Dewey, Roosevelt's opponent in the 1944 Presidential election, conducted himself with political integrity and decorum.

The dissent which was to be commonplace in American society after the war was avoided during the conflict and the American people pursued victory with a steady determination backed by vast material resources (C.1).

THE POSTERS AND THE WAR

When the Great War began in 1914 the era of mass communication had barely begun. It was just two decades since Alfred Northcliffe's *Daily Mail* had proved that a cheap, readable daily newspaper could secure a mass market. There was no radio, no television; the moving picture industry was in its infancy, and, in any case, silent. Posters, therefore, were bound to play a vital role in shaping opinion, providing easily digestible information and boosting morale. Although Britain, Germany, France and the United States boasted a universal literacy many other countries did not. Moreover, even in the most advanced nations a reasonably large proportion of the population did not read all that well.

In these circumstances, the production of eye-catching war posters was an essential ingredient of the war effort. This could present the issues to the public in forceful and simple manner. Stereotyped heroes and villains shouted their messages from the hoardings, God was invoked by both sides (even some saints did double service) and there were blatant appeals to duty, honour, King, Kaiser, and country. Kitchener needed *YOU*, but so did Uncle Sam, and even the Tsar. Indeed, one of the remarkable qualities of World War One posters is the universality of theme, the repetition of exhortation and warning. If fear knows no frontiers, nor, it seems, did many of the posters.

In the Second World War, circumstances had changed and posters could not play the same role as their predecessors. Dozens of inexpensive, well-produced and (in some countries) generally reliable daily or weekly news-papers saturated the market. Millions listened to the radio, both for entertainment and for information. In the United States, Roosevelt became renowned for his broadcast "fire-side chats". Strategically situated radio receivers gave out news to Russian citizens in the streets. Hitler made broadcasting an arm of his foreign policy, and throughout Europe countless listeners tuned in to his speeches during the Czech crisis and Munich.

When Britain "stood alone" the radio speeches of Winston Churchill were extremely effective in bridging the gaps of class and culture, and in generating a feeling of national purpose. In this situation posters produced by the Ministry of Information and other ministries served to reiterate these themes, and to provide essential and useful items of information. On the one hand Churchill could exhort his people, as in *Let us Go Forward Together* (2.2), while a less high-flown but perhaps more practical poster reminded the public that *Doctor Carrot Guards Your Health* (6.3). The other nations at war put their graphic designers and artists to similar work. The results were sometimes brilliant, sometimes banal, but nearly always revealing.

Posters for Home Consumption
The posters of the belligerent nations reveal the inevitable similarities of approach as well as the enormous divergences of assumption and prejudice. Archetypal heroes fix the middle distance with keen (and generally blue) eyes; their square jaws and brawny forearms transcend loyalties and ideologies. Women engaged in active wartime service are brisk and businesslike whether in *Die Schöne Aufgabe* (The Noble Task) (3.1), or in Treidler's *My Girl's a Wow* (3.4) produced for the U.S. Army Ordnance Department. Sometimes whole families march steadfastly to war as in Martha Sawyer's *China; First to Fight!* (C.20).

Flags retained their enormous emotive power. A Japanese poster, *Until We Attack and Win* (C.21) shows an aggressive and well-equipped soldier trampling on the British and United States' flags. A Canadian soldier stands before a defiant Union Jack in *Lets Go Canada!* (C.34). The Stars and Stripes has particular significance, and comprises almost the whole poster in *Give it Your Best* (2.12). A bomb marked *More Production* plunges into an amalgam of the flag of the rising sun and the German swastika (C.12). The hammer and sickle on its scarlet background is both a hideous threat in Nazi and collaborationist posters, and a source of inspiration for Soviet heroes.

God plays a substantially smaller part in the posters of World War Two than in the Great War. His saints hardly make an appearance at all. When the Christian cross appears it is more often than not to mark a grave, of friend or foe. Occasionally the cross is juxtaposed with the Nazi crooked cross. In one poster the Christian Bible is speared by the crude dagger of fascist aggression (C.23). Generally, however, the gods of World War Two propaganda are *Production*, *National Security* or *Industrial Safety*!

But in the beginning there was the god of *Recruitment*! United States'
recruitment posters beckon the civilian, either urgently as in *The U.S.
Marines Want You* (1.6), or more quietly and democratically as in Flagg's
Want Action? Join the U.S. Marine (1.5). Or the patriot's heart strings are
tugged by the angelic liberty figure and the row of American soldiers from
Revolution to Pearl Harbour in Woodburn's *The United States Army: Then—
Now—Forever* (1.7), while Holme's comic-strip girlie appeals to the pocket,
announcing *I Can Save up to a Hundred Dollars Every Two Months Now—Joe's in
the Glider Troops* (1.8). The British Navy rather more phlegmatically *Guards
the Freedom of All* (1.2) in Frank Mason's poster, and a downright gloomy and
unimaginative German poster recruits for the S.S. (1.4).

Having caught one's recruit one can then try to keep up morale. A British
poster explains to anti-aircraft gunners how to *Bring Down Those Aircraft*
(1.12). The British artillery man is reminded in Chapman's poster that
Camouflage Nets Baffle the Hun (1.10). A somewhat goulish Japanese poster
issued by the Handicapped Veterans' Protection Institute asks the civilian to
Extend Aid to the Injured Soldiers (1.14). The American designer Vernon Grant
was keener on prevention than after-care and exhorted a naked G.I.:
Don't Be a Jerk—Don't Get a Mosquito Bayonet in Your . . . (1.13).

Nationalist propaganda and calls for national solidarity were prominent
themes in posters, and national heroes were relied on frequently to convey the
message. In one poster Mussolini and King Victor Emmanuel III present a
battery of noble profiles to the onlooker (2.3), Winston Churchill smiles
benignly as Hurricane fighters swarm round his homburg hat and the public
is reminded of the resolution to *Go Forward Together* (2.2). In Henri Guignon's
Holding the Line, Churchill appears in macabre guise as the head on the British
bulldog (2.6). Morale was, presumably, uplifted by this. So too by a somewhat
idealised representation of Roosevelt, Churchill, Stalin and Chiang Kai-shek
in Harrington's poster printed in Britain. Oddly Chiang's features seem
positively European; Stalin's head has a benign and noble tilt (2.7). Hitler
stares rather mournfully from a German poster (2.1), and Dr. Goebbels'
words are reproduced, ordering *Peasants and Soldiers Stand Together Hand in
Hand to Give the People Their Daily Bread and Safeguard the Freedom of the Reich*
(2.17).

More vigorously a German fist smashes John Bull and his allies to dust in
Into the Dust with All Enemies of Great Germany (2.22). The allied soldiers of
America, France and Britain spring forward in *On Les Aura* (Let Them Have
It!) (2.25), a slogan lifted straight from a famous French poster of World War
One. An American sailor shakes a fist and promises to *Avenge December 7*
(Pearl Harbour) (2.27). Russian soldiers and resistance fighters thrust
bayonets at the Nazis. The Japanese scurry away from a giant-like Chinese
soldier in *The More We Fight the Stronger We Grow. The More the Enemy Fight the
Weaker they Grow* (2.14).

The battle for production was an essential poster theme for the major

33

combatants. A Fougasse poster, *Quick—You're Gaining on Him* (4.12), injects some light relief into the facts and figures of the production war as British factory workers pursue Georing. More seriously a Japanese worker brandishes a hammer (4.13), and a Russian youth points to the industrial might flowering under Stalin and Lenin's lofty example (4.1). An American worker, posed like some mediaeval knight against the Stars and Stripes, shows that *Free Labour Will Win* (4.9). Countless war planes zoom out of the head of Roosevelt, crowned with a victorious V (4.10). A German worker and technician clasp hands in *Wir bleiben Kameraden* (We Remain Comrades) (4.6) and American production soldiers are urged to *Keep the Home Fires Burning* in another comic-strip of a poster (4.15).

Security and safety was essential to production and to civilian morale. A European spy peers through a torn Japanese poster (5.3), while a Japanese intelligence officer picks up gossip from Australia in *The Enemy Listens. Your Words are his Weapons.* (5.11). Jac Leonard reminds Canadians that *The Walls Have Ears* (5.10) and Captain Lacoste's simple but effective *Tittle Tattle Lost the Battle* (5.6) shows Hitler (not for the last time) eavesdropping under the table. Abram Games shows with brilliant graphic effect that *Your Talk May Kill Comrades* (5.15). George Pitot's poster asks simply *Qui a trop parlé?* (Who talked too much?) (5.18).

Safety was something else. The Germans were reminded that *Der Feind Sieht Dein Licht! Verdunken!* (The Enemy Sees Your Light. Blackout!) (5.25), as a hag-ridden R.A.F. bomber bears down on a lighted door. Female British factory workers were told in a poster appropriately reminiscent of Russian social realist art to *Cover Your Hair For Safety. Your Russian Sister Does!* (5.26). Pat Keely's poster said plainly enough, *Splinters are Poisoned Arrows. Get First Aid.* (5.28). After safety, public health was a major concern. Particularly in Britain civilians were urged to *Clean Your Teeth the Right Way* (6.2) or to *Grow Your Own Food* (6.7). The virtues of green vegetables and salads in helping the consumer resist infection were stressed. Since one could aid the war effort by looking after one's teeth and skin, other parts of the body should not be neglected. Hence Games' spine-chilling warning against venereal disease and the casual pick-up in *Hello boy friend, coming MY way?* (6.9).

War finance provided another fruitful theme for posters. Roland Ansieau's *Bons de la Libération à intérèt progressif* peep out of Madelaine's revolutionary bonnet (7.3). Children's paintings are utilized to advertise National Savings, and thus to encourage adults to *Buy More Nails for Hitler's Coffin* (7.4). The *On Les Aura* image emerges yet again in an American effort to boost the Fourth War Loan (7.6). Similarly Norman Rockwell's poster argued that to *Save Freedom of Worship* one should *Buy War Bonds* (7.1).

Posters for the Enemy and the Conquered

But if one great branch of poster propaganda was to boost the home front, another was to attack and vilify the enemy. Nazi propaganda found it convenient, and no doubt effective, to link Jew and Bolshevik together as twin demons. A prewar German poster *The Eternal Jew* (8.1) was a grotesque attempt to associate the Jews with usury, cruelty, and communism. *Victory or Bolshevism!* (Sieg oder Bolschewismus) (8.3) shows a roughly dressed Russian with stereotyped Jewish features. Conquered Belgium was regaled with *Voici Les Soviets* (Here are the Soviets) (8.5) in 1943, where a bearded, inanely-smiling Jew lurks behind the mask of a Russian face. A semitic John Bull lurches across at alert Belgian collaborators in another poster (8.6). More absurd still is a Vichy French poster showing the three zones of global Jewish influence—a three way split, apparently, between the Russian, American and British Jews (8.4).

Ridiculing the enemy and also rendering him ominous was a universal propaganda need. A series of brilliantly effective Russian posters depict Hitler as a variety of mangy and unclean beasts being driven back by the Red Army (9.4, 9.5). Others produced in Russia leave no doubt as to the fate of civilians in Nazi occupied territory (9.6). A British *War Pictorial* poster showed the difference between the German warrior of myth and of reality (9.2). More explicitly, Gee's death's head poster warns *Goebbels Says "Russia First—Britain Next"* (9.3). If Germany could talk of zones of Jewish influence, Britain could illustrate the inexorable nature of German war aims (C.2). Though Hitler, Goering and Mussolini provided easy targets for British humour (for example the Bulmer Cider Ugly Mug poster (9.10)), so, especially in the early years of the war, did Churchill, and later Roosevelt. In this respect *I have helped the Norwegians* (9.11), and *The Two Neptunes* (9.13) are amusing caricatures.

In occupied Europe, the Nazis tried to make collaboration respectable. There were appeals to local traditions, invitations to join the S.S., even tempting inducements to work in Germany, as in *Nous Partons Travailler en Allemagne* (10.1). For those who did not cooperate there was the discomfiture of Mr. Prikkeldraad (10.4), or the sharper fate of Robert Deregnaucourt, executed by a firing squad in January 1941 (10.9). For their part, the Allies could at least release a flood of propaganda posters and leaflets into occupied Europe—for Dutch, Poles, Greeks, Belgians, French, and for all the nations occupied by the Axis powers (11.3, 11.7).

Some Posters in Particular
A number of the posters collected in this book should be commented on for their interest, both from the point of view of graphic design and of subject matter.

Soldiers, Free us from Fascist Oppression (2.41)
This is strongly reminiscent of German Expressionist film posters of the early 1920s—although the two figures are idealized in a characteristically Soviet way.

Produce more Tanks . . . Everything for the Front! Everything for Victory! by El Lissitzky (4.8)
El Lissitzky, the most brilliant of twentieth century Russian designers was a painter, an architect, a typographer and a photographer, and despite the changes in artistic style which were dictated by Stalin insisted on maintaining his uncompromising individuality. A pioneer of the technique of "Photomontage", El Lissitzky here uses it in an impressive poster, where several images are juxtaposed yet create a powerful impression.

We Drink the Water of our Native Dneiper . . . (2.45)
Resembles a film poster. The Russians dramatised war without suppressing its dreadful reality.

Soldiers save these children from death by starvation (9.6)
A situation that is used frequently in war propaganda. The idealization of one's own side and the representation of the enemy as a brute is typical of many war posters. This Russian poster exhibits a very high degree of professionalism; the quality of its imagery is that of an Eisenstein film.

We Remain Comrades in the German Workers' Front (4.6)
The faceless quality of Nazi and Fascist art is demonstrated in this crude and surprisingly amateur poster. Certain elements from Expressionism survive in vernacular form.

The Dutch Fight on to Victory (11.3)
Vigorous and almost balletic—a tradition inherited from English and French poster design of the early thirties—contrast it with the monumentality of many German posters.

Want Action? Join U.S. Marine Corps! (1.5)
An appeal to the instincts of comradeship and the desire for glory. In style and sentiment a poster that could have come from the First World War.

The U.S. Marines Want You. Enlist Today (1.6)
An innocent and effective poster, part of the American tradition of popular art—later to be seized upon by the Pop school in the late 1950s and early 1960s. Probably based on the classic British First World War poster: *Your Country Needs You.*

I Can Save up to a Hundred Dollars every Two Months Now . . . Joe's in the Glider Troops (1.8)
One wonders whether this design is a sophisticated attempt at naivety or whether it is the genuine article. One sees the style that the Pop school, particularly Roy Lichtenstein, have transformed into a new vocabulary.

36

Give 'em Both Barrels by Jean Carlu (4.7)
Jean Carlu worked in England during the thirties. This poster appears to borrow C. R. W. Nevinson's (1889-1946) disturbing image of the machine-gunners in his painting "La Mitrailleuse" (1915).

Long Live the Duce, Founder of the Empire (2.3)
The grouping of posters together is a characteristically Italian method of display. The posters themselves lack conviction and imagination – this may even represent an unconscious form of protest by the designer!

Let us Go Forward Together (2.2)
A photo-montage (compare with El Lissitzky's powerful but tense poster) – Churchill is shown as firm and purposeful – not as a sub-deity like Hitler or Mussolini.

Grow Your Own Food by Abram Games (6.7)
Complex imagery rendered in a forceful style. Typical of the best work of the Official artists.

Your Talk may Kill Your Comrades (1942) by Abram Games (5.15)
One of Games' most important and successful posters using the complex style favoured by British official propaganda.

Talk Kills (1942) by Abram Games (5.14)
Two powerful images are opposed in a way that is reminiscent of the montage technique of the film. One of the most effective posters of the Second World War.

You Know a Vital Secret – Keep it Dark by Lewitt-Him (Jan Lewitt and George Him) (5.16)
Issued on the eve of the invasion this poster is the joint work of two Polish designers who came to England in the late thirties as refugees. The mild tone (not to alienate factory workers) contrasts with Games' "Talk Kills" poster.

Hello Boy Friend, Coming MY Way? by Reginald Mount (6.9)
A spine-chilling and efficient design – frank and without ambiguity. The image is again complex and literary in the manner of the best British work.

Please pass Down the Car by Fougasse (Kenneth Bird) (6.5)
A gentle hinting rather than an exhortation characterizes much of the propaganda intended for Londoners. Fougasse's work, now strangely dated, was intended to appeal to the *Punch*-reading City worker, and was immensely popular.

37

Doctor Carrot Guards Your Health (6.4)
Like "Potato Pete"–another anthropomorphic vegetable–"Dr. Carrot" was a half serious creation, but the publicity for the humble carrot was part of a brilliantly mounted campaign to encourage the use of home-grown foods.

War Pictorial (9.2)
This example of poster-journalism uses the format pioneered in England by *Picture Post* and is for careful reading rather than the casual glance. Crude Nazi war paintings of idealised Aryan fighting men are contrasted with the wretched faces of defeat. The text is oddly pompous.

Qui a Trop Parlé . . . by Georges Pitot (5.18)
Reminiscent of the style of the brilliant cartoonist Paul Iribe of *Le Mot* (the daring French magazine of the first year of the 1914 War, publication of which was stopped as a result of official pressure), this poster has, somehow, an air of futility–unforgiveable in the convention of the war poster.

Replace Guards by Lee-Elliott (5.27)
A factory poster which uses the bold style pioneered by E. McKnight Kauffer in the 1920s and which became the dominant influence in English poster design.

Journée Franco-Britannique (2.15)
By the 1930s English and French poster design had adopted a similar style–less intense and using less ambitious typography than the German. This poster from the phoney-war period resembles the Shell posters of the thirties and seems to lack conviction.

Un Seul Combat Pour une Seule Patrie by Knopf (11.7)
Like the British war posters this uses a complex imagery (the traditional helmet of Liberté, the Cross of Lorraine, the civilian, the soldier, Paris, North Africa)–but without the same powerful effect.

The Polish Relief Fund by M. Zulawski (11.5)
A conventional and almost classical war poster subsituting the proud standard for the brave battle-stained one, the typography–characteristic of the period–seems to have been influenced by English contemporary design.

Give it Your Best! (2.12)
The best American designs utilise the vernacular tradition, the style of the carnival or the parade. Painted at the height of the vogue for Pop, Jasper Johns' pictures consisted simply of the United States' flag.

A Careless Word . . . Another Cross by John Atherton (5.17)
British war posters had a widespread influence on all the Allied governments—
this moving poster is an excellent example of the style pioneered by Abram
Games and is quite outside the American tradition of the time.

In 1942 America will Build 60,000 War Planes (4.10)
Ingenious use of the "Victory V" symbol to provide a perspective framework
for a terrifying cavalcade of Flying Fortress bombers. A nightmarish image.

Protect his Future . . . Watch Your Tongue by Earl Christy (5.13)
A straightforward appeal to the sentiments. Stylistically a poster reminiscent
of American design in the 1920s.

Until We Attack and Win (C.21)
The Japanese soldier is shown as a modern Samurai warrior, in the full dress
of his trade. This poster has a genuine heroic quality that distinguishes it from
the Nazi posters; it is much closer in spirit to the Russian ones.

Military Affairs are of Prime Importance : Victory is of Prime Importance (2.5)
China obviously lacked the sophisticated publicity machine of the other
warring nations, but in this poster effective use is made of the traditional
Chinese idiom, although the influence of Western publicity is strongly evident.

Kick out the Germans (C.13)
Contrast this brilliant Italian Partisan poster with the banalities of fascist
propaganda; in style it resembles Italian postwar publicity.

Let's Give Him Enough and on Time designed by Norman Rockwell (C.10)
Uses the powerful machine-gun image that C. R. W. Nevinson used in "La
Mitrailleuse" (1915). Rockwell's technique became unfashionable for a time,
but he is now seen as a major artist.

Your Britain—Fight For It Now by Frank Newbould (C.27)
Quite outside the mainstream of war posters with its romantic vision of the
England of William Blake. Newbould produced distinguished work for the
G.P.O., who were the patrons of many of the best poster designers, in the
1930s.

Your Britain—Fight For It Now by Abram Games (C.3)
The new arising from the ruins of the past is the theme of this optimistic poster
with its rather literary imagery.

We French Workers warn You . . . by Ben Shahn (C.17)
Ben Shahn, the leading member of the America school of social realism,

developed a unique style of propaganda poster with images rather like those of certain postwar social realist films.

Guinness is Good For You (Designers: S. H. Benson Ltd.) (6.1)
An outstandingly effective poster, full of wry humour, and with an unambiguous message. Inevitably commercial advertising during the War made heavy use of the wartime themes which touched so large a number of the population. This poster has hardly dated.

Bulmer's Cider (9.10)
A gently humorous verse pokes fun at Hitler and his "ugly mug". In the early stages of the war the Nazi leaders had not yet attained the awesome and even horrific stature that was later to characterize them in the public eye.

Thank You Foster Parents. We Want More Like You (5.2)
Agent: Mather and Crowther for Ministry of Health Evacuation Campaign. Perhaps less sophisticated technically than the work of the official poster artists, but still very striking and calculated to arouse strong emotions. Its title has a rueful quality about it, since quite large numbers of the better-off homes in Britain avoided taking in evacuees.

Victory at Any Cost (2.16)
The stultifying effect that the Nazis had on all forms of design, whether it was architecture, graphic, or painting, is epitomised in this gross attempt at creating an image of heroism. Nazi posters in general were unrealistic, wooden and somehow lacking in conviction.

Because Somebody Talked by Wesley (1943) (C.33)
A sentimental appeal (no doubt an effective one) with a bereaved spaniel that recalls that classic of Victorian narrative *The Shepherd's Last Mourner*.

A New Fish Dish—Fresh Salted Cod (C.26)
Strong line and colour tries to sell the British public a hitherto uncoveted fish dish. Presumably the hungry shoppers were not supposed to notice the contradiction of "fresh" and "salted" in the poster.

For Freedom and Life—the Volksturm (The German equivalent to the Home Guard) by M. Jetnir (2.33)
The young and the old stand shoulder to shoulder in defence of the Fatherland. Though the face presented to the advancing enemy is meant to be heroic, there is more than a hint of despair and pathos in fighting for a now lost cause. In fact the *Volksturm*, when put to the test, were of little use unless supported by units of the *Wermacht*.

One People, One State, One Leader (2.1)
Hitler is idealistically portrayed as a steady, far-sighted visionary, dreaming no doubt of *lebensraum*, certainly of the Reich that was to last for a thousand years.

A.R.P. Calling You. Get in Touch with your Local Council by Pat Keely (1938) (5.12)
A stylish poster, typical of the 1930s. The sounding siren could equally belong to a Toytown Train.

Buying the Meat of Illegally Slaughtered Cattle is a Crime (C.22)
The greedily grasping hand is a conventional image of guilt. The Allies did all they could to encourage the Black Market in German occupied territory.

Churchill as an Octopus (9.7)
This caricature of the octopus Churchill, dripping blood at the end of his tentacles, uses the famous cigar in the same way as anti-semitic and anti-capitalist propaganda – to suggest ruthless rapacity.

Bits of Careless Talk are Pieced Together By the Enemy (C.28)
A striking, ingenious and effective poster. The swastika ring on the menacing hand suggests not only the enemy but also decadence.

Posters of World War Two

1. Recruitment and Morale Boosting

RÉPUBLIQUE FRANÇAISE

Modèle 8001 b.

RAPPEL IMMÉDIAT

DE

CERTAINES CATÉGORIES DE RÉSERVISTES

Par ordre du Ministre de la Défense Nationale et de la Guerre et du Ministre de l'Air, les officiers, sous-officiers et hommes de troupe des réserves porteurs d'un ordre ou fascicule de mobilisation de couleur blanche portant en surcharge le chiffre «8» (voir modèle au bas de cette affiche) se mettront en route immédiatement et sans délai sans attendre une notification individuelle.

Ils rejoindront le lieu de convocation indiqué sur leur ordre ou fascicule de mobilisation dans les conditions précisées par ce document.

Le   19   heures.

Les Ministres de la Défense Nationale et de la Guerre et de l'Air.

IMPRIMERIE NATIONALE

1.1 *French*
"Immediate Call-Up of Certain Categories of Reservists."
Issued on 28th September, 1939, twenty-five days after the outbreak of war.

1.2 *British* (Frank H. Mason)
(above left)
A solid and dignified poster in the
best traditions of the Royal Navy.

1.3 *American* (Tom Woodburn)
(above right)
The stripes of the "stars and stripes"
are angry red lightning flashes of
belligerency.

1.4 *German* (Mjülnir)
"Waffen-S.S. – Join up as soon as
you are eighteen. Short or long-
term service." A gloomy and
uninviting poster.

1.5 *American*
(James Montgomery Flagg)
Strongly reminiscent of the
First World War posters designed
by this distinguished artist.

1.6 *American*
Not far removed from the
First World War poster
Your Country Needs You!

1.7 *American* (Tom Woodburn) Another United States appeal to the flag, and to a brief, but not inglorious, military history.

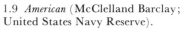

1.9 *American* (McClelland Barclay; United States Navy Reserve).

1.10 *British* (W. R. Chapman) Issued by the Ministry of Supply.

1.11 *British* (Frank Newbould) During the Blitz the Auxiliary Fire Service were one of the most vital arms of national defence.

1.12 *British*
An official guide for anti-aircraft
gunners.

BRING DOWN THOSE AIRCRAFT

DON'T GET FLUSTERED. ALLOW A 12 DEGREE LEAD
AND SWING. THE AIRCRAFT IS UNLIKELY TO DROP
AT YOUR FEET, BUT WILL FALL OUT OF YOUR SIGHT,
IF YOU AIM CORRECTLY. YOU MUST ENGAGE IT.

NOTE. ARMOURED POSITIONS ARE SHOWN IN RED

ALL OTHER PARTS ARE VULNERABLE TO SMALL ARMS FIRE.

1.13 *American* (Vernon Grant) The advances in medical science drastically reduced the number of American troops who died of disease in World War Two.

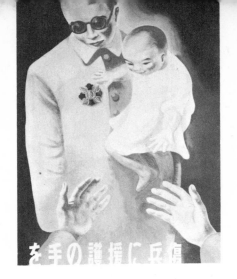

1.14 *Japanese*
"Extend Aid to the Injured Soldiers."

復兵に援護の手を

1.15 *German/Austrian*
"Wounded! The Fatherland thanks you. But never forget that you are representatives of the Front. Impeccable behaviour is a matter of honour!" (Issued by the *Wehrmachtkommandant*, Vienna).

Verwundete!

Die Heimat dankt Euch.

Denkt aber daran, daß Ihr Vertreter der Front seid.

Vorbildliche Haltung ist daher Ehrensache!

Hierzu gehört:

1. **Vorsicht bei Gesprächen – Feind hört mit!**

2. **Soldatisches Verhalten überall, wo Ihr Euch aufhaltet!**
   Tadellose Haltung!   Vorschriftsmäßiger Anzug!

3. **Ehrenbezeigungen rechtzeitig und straff!**
   Auch in geschlossenen Räumen. Auf die Art der Verwundung wird Rücksicht genommen. Aber Verwundung befreit nicht von Ehrenbezeigung.

4. **Nicht betrinken!**
   Trunkenheit schädigt das Ansehen der Wehrmacht!

5. **Den Befehlen der Wehrmachtstreifen ist sofort zu gehorchen.**

Tretet in der Öffentlichkeit so auf,
daß Euch die Achtung und Verehrung sicher bleibt.

Der Wehrmachtkommandant von Wien.

Wehrkreisdruckerei XVII, Wien, II.968. – Q 0349

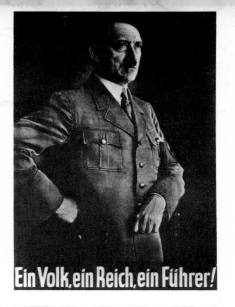

2.1 *German*
"One People, One Country,
One Leader!"

Ein Volk, ein Reich, ein Führer!

2. Patriotic Posters

"LET US
GO FORWARD
TOGETHER"

2.2 *British*
A photo-montage.

2.3 *Italian*
Wall posters of Mussolini and
King Victor Emmanuel III.

2.4 *Italian*
A prewar Italian propaganda
poster-cum- news-sheet (*To the
Peasants*), printed in the fifteenth
year (1937) of Mussolini's
accession to power.

2.5 *Chinese*
"Military affairs
are of prime
importance:
Victory is of prime
importance."

HOLDING THE LINE!

2.8 *Japanese* (right top)
"Nippon" or "Japan". An appeal
to Japanese traditionalism.

2.9 *Japanese* (right bottom)
Extols the Japanese youth
movement.

2.10 *Chinese* (far right)
"As long as the enemy aggression
goes on so long will we not rest in
our war of resistance." (Poster
made by the Political Section of
the Military Commission.)

2.6 *American* (Henri Guignon)
Portrays Churchill (and Britain)
as America's first line of defence.

2.7 *British* (G. Harrington)
Idealised Allied leaders.

FRANKLIN D. ROOSEVELT

WINSTON S. CHURCHILL

JOSEPH STALIN

CHIANG KAI-SHEK

本 ENIPPON

青年徒步旅行

敵人侵略一旦止，
我們抗戰一日休！
軍事委員會政治部製

2.11 *Greek*
"America Calling". A pro-German poster satirising Roosevelt's reports regarding the progress of the war.

2.12 *American*
Issued by the Office of War Information.

2.13 *French*
"This is what awaits us if the government is incapable of getting French aviation out of the mess caused by the Popular Front!" A prewar poster aimed at the Daladier government.

VOILA CE QUI NOUS ATTEND, SI LE GOUVERNEMENT N'EST PAS CAPABLE DE SORTIR L'AVIATION FRANÇAISE DE LA SITUATION DRAMATIQUE OÙ L'A PLACÉE LE FRONT POPULAIRE!

11.12 NOVEMBRE 1939

★ JOURNÉE FRANCO-BRITANNIQUE ★
AU BÉNÉFICE DE CEUX QUI COMBATTENT ET DE LEURS FAMILLES

2.15 *French*
"Franco-British Day. For the benefit of those who are fighting, and their families."

2.14 *Chinese*
"The more we fight the stronger we grow: The more the enemy fights the weaker they grow."

SIEG UM JEDEN PREIS

JDEPE-Sammelmarken Reihe 2 (1-12) Bild 4

2.16 *German*
"Victory at Any Cost".

65

2.17 *German*
"Peasants and soldiers stand together hand in hand to give the people their daily bread and to safeguard the freedom of the Reich."
(Dr. Goebbels.)

2.18 *Japanese*
Posters glorifying the Japanese air force.

2.19 *German*
"Raw materials From our own colonies!"
Issued by the Colonial Federation, a body aiming to re-settle African colonies "lost" after the 1st World War.

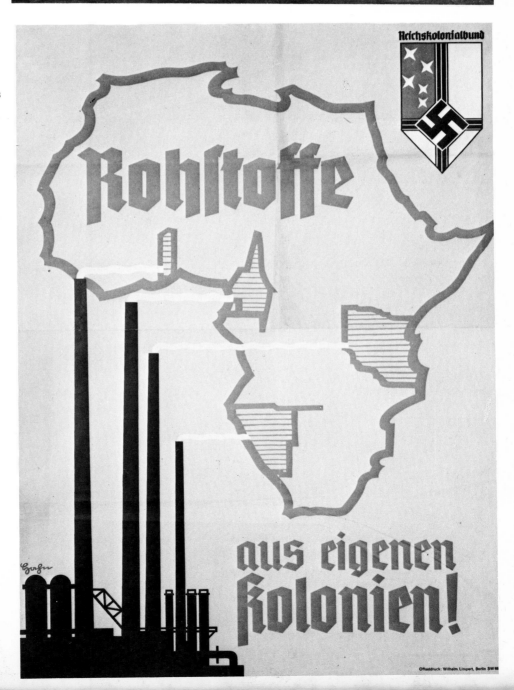

2.20 *German*
"I have perceived that with
courage and will-power one
can overcome everything."
(Scharnhorst.)

2.21 *German*
"Hard times
Hard tasks
Hard hearts!"

2.22 *German*
"Into the dust with all
enemies of Greater
Germany!" (Printed for
occupied Belgium.)

2.23 *Italian* (D. Fontana)
"The order to strengthen
the war industry, coming
from the highest authority
in the land, finds Terni perfectly
prepared."
(Terni were an arms
manufacturing company.)

2.24 *American* (Leon Helguera)
An appeal to Latin America.

2.25 *French* (right)
"Let them have it!"
Printed in London, and based on
the famous First World War
poster with the same slogan.

2.26 *American*
Another poster inspired by
"On Les Aura!"

2.27 *American* (Bernard Perkin)
Revenge for Pearl Harbour.

2.28 *American* (**Max Gordon**)
Britain seen, once more, as
America's first line of
defence.

2.29 *British*
A simple juxtaposition of
crosses. Issued by the
Ministry of Information.

I believe . . .

2.32 *American*
Issued by the Office of War
Information, 1943.

Ten years ago:

THE NAZIS BURNED THESE BOOKS

...but free Americans CAN STILL READ THEM

2.33 *German*
"For Liberty and Life—The
Volksturm." (Home Guard.)

2.34 *American*
The United States Army
Recruiting Service emphasises the
national significance of the stars
and stripes.

2.36 *French*
"Between the
hammer and the
anvil."

2.35 *British*
A Ministry of
Information
Exhibition in 1942.

ARTEAU ...

CLUME !..

Great Britain will pursue the WAR AGAINST JAPAN to the very end.

WINSTON CHURCHILL

2.37 *British*
Defiance is hurled
at Japan.

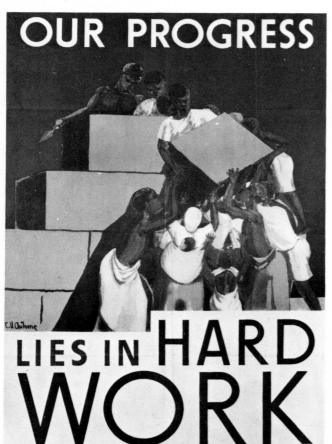

2.38 *British*
An impressive list of British
Crown Colonies, Protectorates
and Mandates.

2.39 *British* (lower left)
(A. V. Asihene) For African
colonial consumption.

2.40 *Russian* (lower right) (Denz)
"A Happy Festival for our street."
An astringent and confident
contrast of images.

2.41 *Russian* (right)
"Soldiers free us from fascist oppression."
(Government Publication *Art*, 1943.)

2.42 *Russian* (lower right)
(Koukrinikci) (1941)
"We will mercilessly shatter and obliterate the enemy." A Soviet soldier confronts Hitler who has just broken the Soviet-Nazi Non Agression Pact.

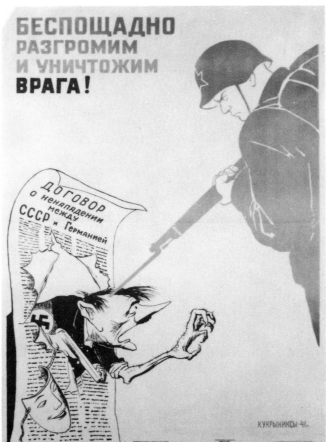

ПРОТЯНЕМ РУКУ БРАТСКОЙ ПОМОЩИ ЖИТЕЛЯМ СЕЛ И ГОРОДОВ, ОСВОБОЖДЕННЫХ ОТ ФАШИСТОВ.

2.43 *Russian* (V. Elkin) (1942)
"We will stretch out a hand
of brotherly help to the
inhabitants of villages and
towns set free from the
fascists."

ОКНО
ТАСС № 890

ПОДАРОК С ВОСТОКА

СТРАНА БУРЯТ-МОНГОЛЬСКАЯ,
ВСТРЕЧАЯ НОВЫЙ ГОД,
ГЕРОЯМ КРАСНОЙ АРМИИ
НА ФРОНТ ПОДАРОК ШЛЕТ.

ФРОНТОВИКОВ ПРИВЕТСТВУЯ,
ЖЕЛАЕТ ИМ ВОСТОК
ДОБИТЬ В БОЯХ НА ЗАПАДЕ
ВРАГА В КРАТЧАЙШИЙ СРОК.

ХУДОЖНИК—П. ШУХМИН   А. ЖАРОВ

2.44 *Russian* (P. Shukhmin)
"A gift from the East.
Happy New Year."
An essay in Soviet solidarity.

2.45 *Russian* (N. Zhukov)
"We drink the water of our native Dneiper. We will drink from the Prut, the Niemen and the Bug. We will clean Soviet soil from fascist impurity."

2.46 *Russian* (V. Ivanov) (1943)
A Russian soldier turns the sign, pointing *East*, to the *West*. The Germans are being driven back.

3. Women in Wartime

3.1 *German*
"The Noble Task."
Recruiting for the womens'
section of a Nazi labour
organisation.

3.3 *British*
Recruiting land
girls.

3.4 *American* (Treidler)
A boost for the Women
Ordnance Workers.

4. The Battle for Greater Production

4.1 *Russian* (A. Kokorekin)
(1942)
"Excel Yourselves
To Produce Better Help for
the Front."

4.2 *British* (1940)
Ernest Bevin (Minister of Labour) appeals for greater exports as Britain stands alone.

4.3 *British*
A postwar production poster, but owing much to the wartime poster idiom.

4.4 *British*
Solidarity at the production front.

4.5 *British*
A well-executed Communist
Party poster that hankers
after the "Second Front."

4.6 *German* (Penern)
"Then and Now We
Remain Comrades. The
German Workers' Front."

4.8 *Russian* (El Lissitzky)
"Produce more tanks, anti-
tank guns, planes, artillery,
mine-sweepers, shells,
machine guns, rifles!
Everything for the Front!
Everything for Victory!"

4.7 *American* (Jean Carlu)

ДАВАЙТЕ ПОБОЛЬШЕ ТАНКОВ, ПРОТИВОТАНКОВЫХ РУЖЕЙ И ОРУДИЙ, САМОЛЕТОВ, ПУШЕК, МИНОМЕТОВ, СНАРЯДОВ, ПУЛЕМЕТОВ, ВИНТОВОК!

ВСЕ ДЛЯ ФРОНТА! ВСЕ ДЛЯ ПОБЕДЫ!

Anton Bruehl Pho[...]

FREE LABOR WILL WIN

WAR PRODUCTION BOARD
WASHINGTON, D.C.   A-15

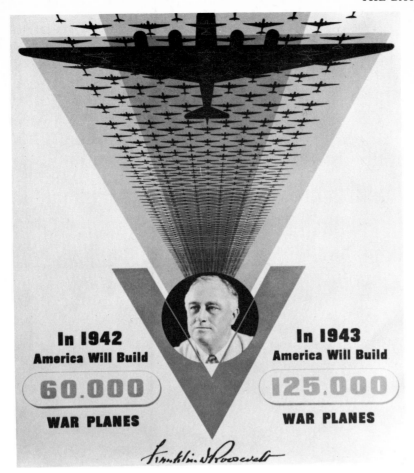

4.9 *American* (far left)
Issued by the War
Production Board, 1942.

4.10 *American* (above left)
The arsenal of democracy.

4.11 *American* (Garrett Bruce)
(1942)

4.12 *British*
(Fougasse – Kenneth Bird)

4.13 *Japanese*
"Labour Mobilization."

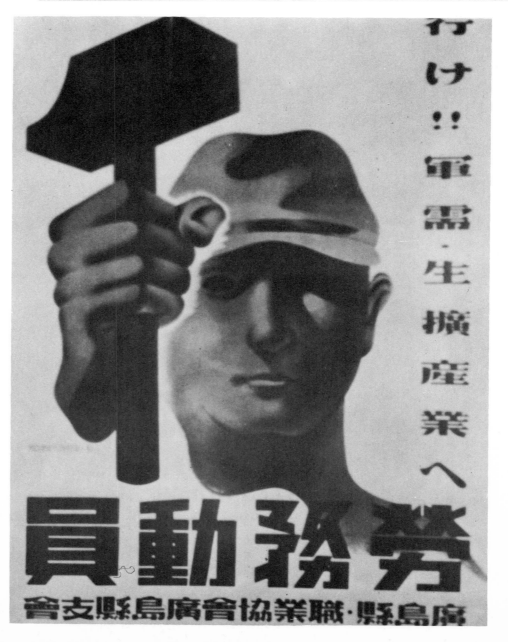

GAINING ON HIM !!

4.14 *German*
"One struggle, one
intention, one destination:
Victory at any Cost."

4.16 *American*
(Cyrus C. Hungerford)

4.17 *American*
(H. Koerner)

5. National Security and Safety

5.1 *British*
A Ministry of Health poster. 105

Thank you, Foster=Parents . . . we want more like you!

Some kindly folk have been looking after children from the cities for over six months. Extra work? Yes, they've been a handful!... but the foster-parents know they have done the right thing.

And think of all the people who have cause to be thanking the foster-parents. First, the children themselves. They're out of a danger-zone — where desperate peril may come at any minute. And they're healthier and happier. Perhaps they don't say it but they certainly mean "Thank you".

Then their parents. Think what it means to them!

The Government are grateful to all the 20,000 people in Scotland who are so greatly helping the country by looking after evacuated children. But many new volunteers are needed—to share in the present task and to be ready for any crisis that may come. Won't you be one of them? All you need do is enrol your name with the local Authority. You will be doing a real service for the nation. You may be saving a child's life.

The Secretary of State, who has been entrusted by the Government with the conduct of evacuation, asks you urgently to join the Roll of those who are willing to receive children. Please apply to your local Council.

5.2 *British*
Issued for the
Ministry of Health
Education
Campaign.

5.3 *Japanese*
"Peoples' Espionage
Prevention Exhibit."

5.4 *British* (G. Lacoste)
(1940)
Captain Lacoste was an
officer in the British forces
in France.

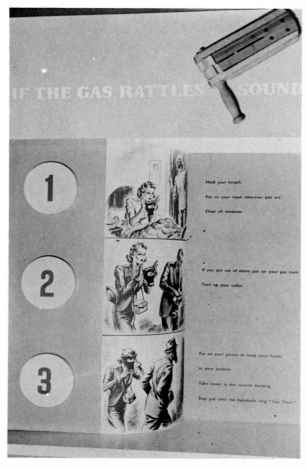

5.5 *British*
In preparation for a gas
attack.

5.6 *British* (G. Lacoste)

5.7 *British* (G. Lacoste)

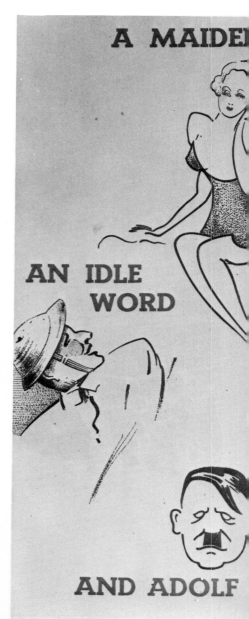

SERVE IN SILENCE · SE TAIRE C'EST SERVIR

5.8 *British* (G. Lacoste)

5.9 *British*

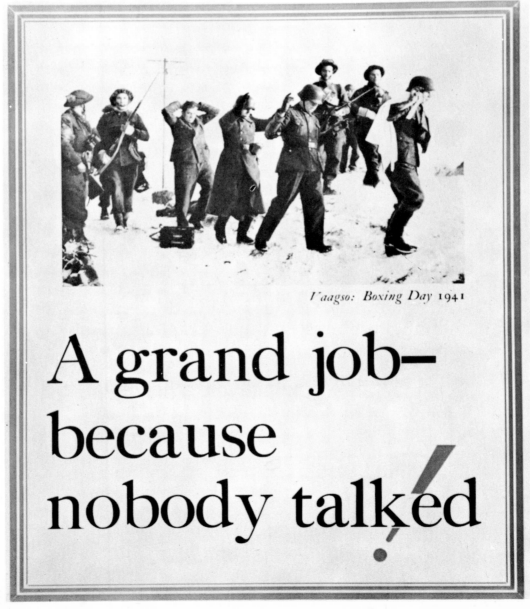

Vaagso: Boxing Day 1941

A grand job–
because
nobody talked!

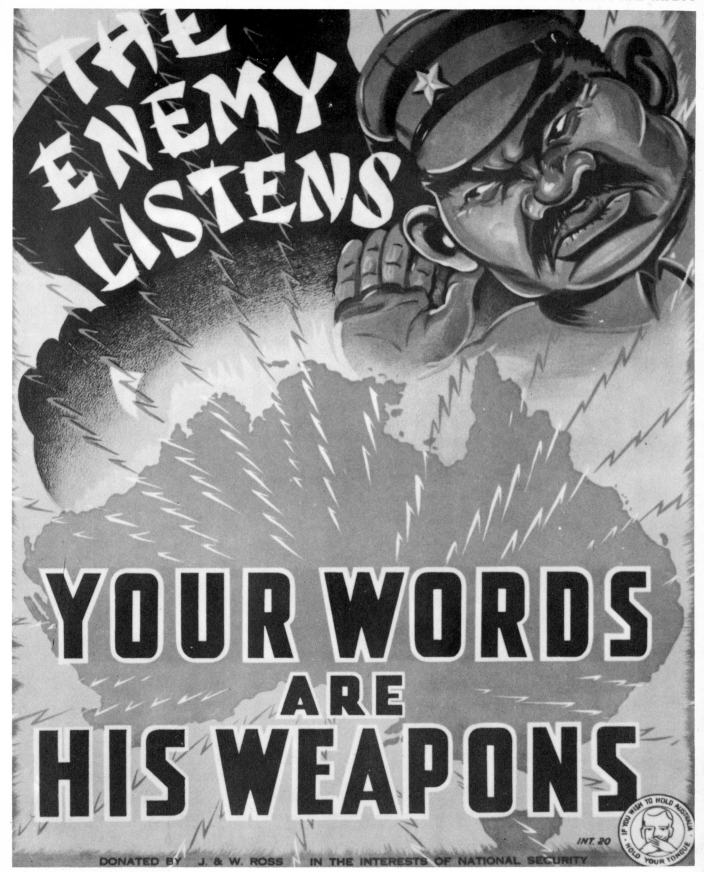

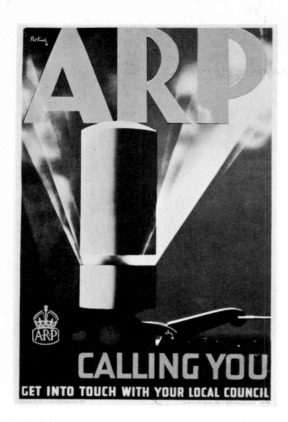

5.12 *British* (above left)
(Pat Keely)
A 1938 precursor of the war.

5.13 *American* (above right)
(Earl Christy)
(1943)

5.14 *British* (Abram Games)
(1942)

5.15 *British* (right)
(Abram Games)
(1942)

5.16 *British*
(Jan Lewitt and
George Him)

a careless word

...another cross

5.17 *American*
(John Atherton)

5.18 *French* (Georges Pitot)
"Who talked too much?"
From the "Phoney War"
period.

5.19 *American*
(Cyrus C. Hungerford)

Poison Gas on the Battlefront is paralyzing. So is propaganda gas on our Production Front. A vicious rumor is one of the Dictators' Deadliest weapons. It starts with a whispering campaign and can do as much harm as an invading army—So Beware of suspicious gossip. Put on a gas mask and walk right through!

You Are A PRODUCTION SOLDIER, America's First Line of Defense is HERE.

SHELTER AT HOME

The New Government

STEEL INDOOR 'TABLE' SHELTER

IS NOW AVAILABLE IN THIS DISTRICT : PARTICULARS FROM

5.20 *British* (opposite)

5.21 *British* (left) (Eckersley)

5.22 *British* (Pat Keely) (1941)

5.23 *Japanese*
"People's Anti-Air Raid Exhibit."

　5.24 *American* (1943)

5.25 *German* (Herweg)
"The Enemy sees your lights!
Blackout!"

5.26 *British* (Gilby)
Anglo-Soviet solidarity is
expressed in this poster.

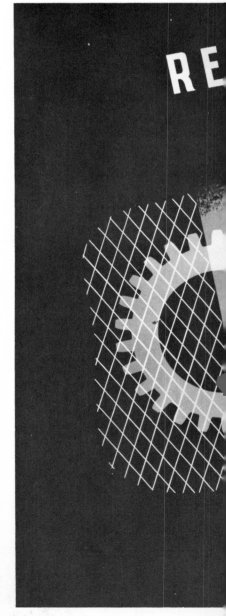

5.27 *British* (Lee Elliot)

SPLINTERS
are poisoned arrows – get First Aid

Issued by the Ministry of Labour and National Service and produced by the Royal Society for the Prevention of Accidents.

5.28 *British* (Pat Keely) (1942)

5.29 *American*
(Cyrus C. Hungerford)

6. The Health of the Nation

6.1 *British* (Designers
S. H. Benson Ltd.)

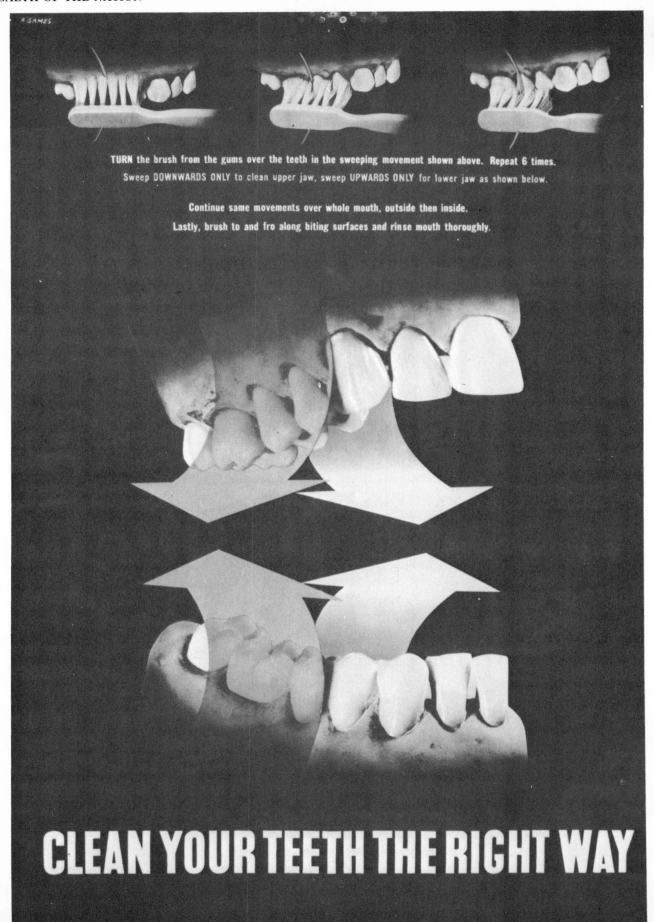

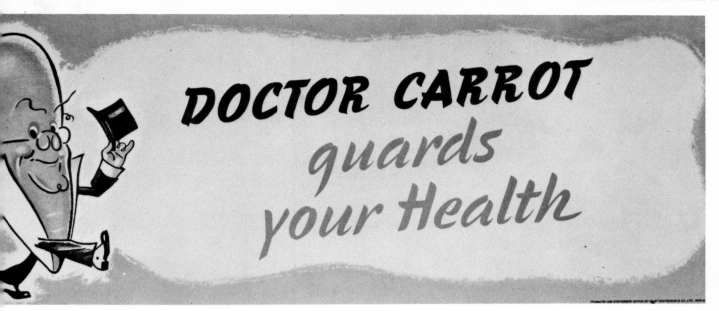

N VEGETABLES & SALADS

ou to resist infection, clear the

nd take the place of raw fruit.

6.2 *British* (opposite)
(Abram Games)

6.4 *British* (above)

6.3 *British* (left)
Produced by the
Ministry of Food

6.5 *British* (Fougasse)

Please pass down the car!

— SOMEDAY YOU MIGHT
WANT TO GET IN, YOURSELF!

Rabbits can be fed on

Hedgerow Weeds · Garden Waste · Kitchen Scraps

Hedge Parsley	Brussels Sprout Stems	Pot Scrapings
Plantain	Lettuce Leaves	Table Scraps
Sow Thistle	Cabbage Leaves	Root Peelings
Dandelion	Waste Potatoes	Fish Waste
Groundsel	Lawn Mowings	Pea Pods

6.6 *British* (left) (Henrigh).

6.7 *British* (Abram Games)

6.8 *British* (Abram Games).

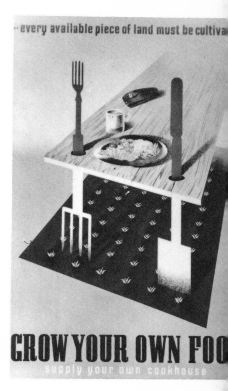

6.9 *British* (Reginald Mount)

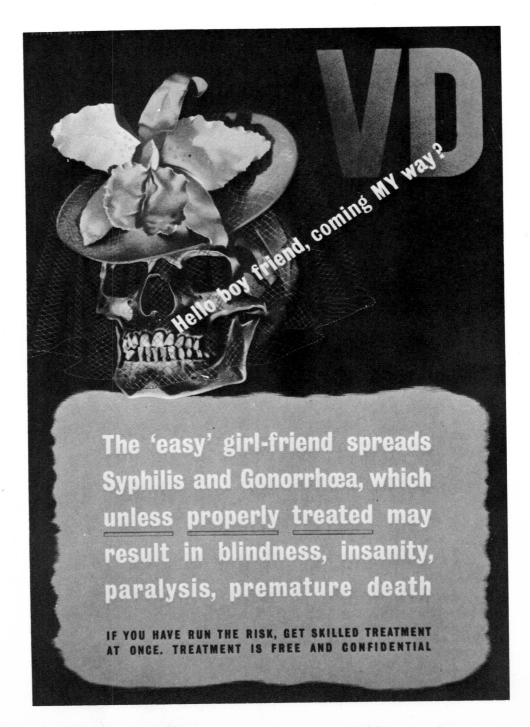

7. War Finance

7.1 *American* (Norman Rockwell)

131

7.2 *British*
Children's poster.

7.3 *French* (Roland Ansieau)
(1945)

7.4 *British*
Children's posters.

7.5 *British* (Rothholz) (1943)

7.6 *American* (1943)
A U.S. Treasury version of
"On Les Aura!"

8. Anti-Semitism

8.1 *German* (1937)
"The eternal Jew"
This poster illustrates a
favourite Nazi identification
of the Jewish people with
bolshevism.

135

WENN·ES·DEM
INTERNATIO/
NALEN·FINANZJUDEN/
TUM·GELINGEN
SOLLTE/DIE·VÖLKER
NOCH·EINMAL·IN
EINEN·WELTKRIEG
ZU·STÜRZEN/DANN
WIRD·DAS·ERGEB/
NIS·NICHT·DER·SIEG
DES·JUDENTUMS
SEIN·SONDERN DIE
VERNICHTUNG·DER·JÜ
DISCHEN·RASSE IN
EUROPA

ADOLF HITLER

WOCHENSPRUCH DER NSDAP. / HERAUSGEBER REICHSPROPAGANDALEITUNG / FOLGE 37, 7.-13. SEPTEMBER 1941
ZENTRALVERLAG DER NSDAP. MÜNCHEN

8.2 *German*
"Should the international Jewish financiers succeed again in plunging the nations into a World War, the result will be not the victory of the Jews but the annihilation of the whole Jewish race in Europe." Adolf Hitler.

8.3 *German*
"Victory or Bolshevism!"

8.4 *French*
"The partition of the world into three zones of Jewish influence." An example of anti-semitic propaganda for occupied France.

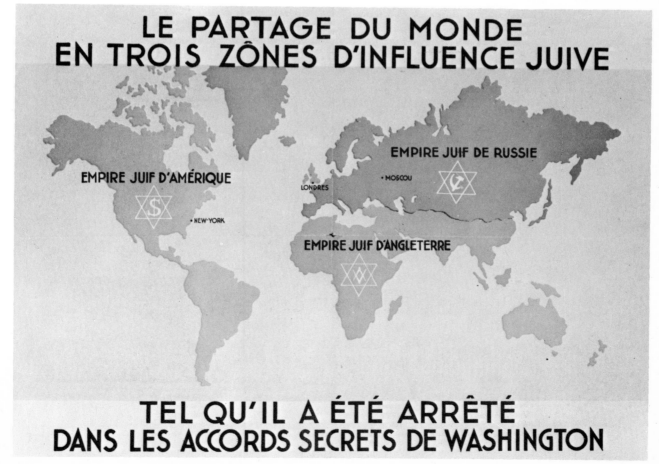

8.5 *Belgian* (1943)
"Here are the Soviets."
An equation between Jews and
bolsheviks for an anti-Russian
exhibition in occupied Brussels.

8.7 *Belgian*
"Against bolshevism!
Join the Walloon Legion."
Some numbers of Belgians fought
with the German army on the
eastern front.

8.6 *Belgian*
The Flemish collaborationist reply
to the British menace is "Our
answer – Ready with the gun!"

8.8 *Danish* "For Denmark! Against Bolshevism!" Danish collaborationist poster.

9. The Enemy Abused and Satirised

9.2 *British*
A war pictorial.

9.3 *British* (Gee)

9.4 *Russian*
"The Story of the Fisherman and the Fish."
Taking its title from a Russian fairy tale, this poster ridicules Hitler's desire for a separate peace with Britain and the United States.

9.5 *Russian*
"Those who may try to
attack will come up against
shattering resistance. Let
them not put their pig's
snout into the Soviet
Kitchen garden." (Stalin.)

9.6 *Russian* (V. Koretsky)
"Soldiers save these children
from death by starvation.
Exterminate the German
bandits."

9.7 *French*
A collaborationist view of
Churchill.

9.8 *Russian*
A satire on the "dirty lap dog
Fifi." (Pierre Laval, the leader of
Vichy France).

И В ТОТ ЖЕ ДЕНЬ
НЕМЕЦКИЙ ДОГ,
КОТОРЫЙ ФРАНЦИЮ СТЕРЕГ,
ЗАЛАЯЛ ЯРОСТНЕЙ,
ЧЕМ РАНЬШЕ,
ЧТОБ СЛЫШНО БЫЛО
НА ЛАМАНШЕ:

— ГАВ, ГАВ! ПАРИЖСКИЙ НАШ ПАРАД
ПРОДЛИЛСЯ ДВА ЧАСА ПОДРЯД!

БОЛОНКА ГРЯЗНАЯ ФИФИ
ИЗ АГЕНСТВА ГАВАС — ОФИ
В ОТВЕТ ПРОЛАЯЛА ПОЖИЖЕ:
— ДА, ДА ПАРАД! У НАС В ПАРИЖЕ!

9.10 *British*
One way to sell cider!

9.9 *Russian* (Koukrinikci)
"Overall Mobilisation in
Germany! He will do. Next one!"

9.11 *German*
Propaganda for British
consumption!

9.12 *Dutch* (right)
A list of British wrongs against the
Dutch, beginning with the first
Anglo-Dutch War (1652-4) and
including the Boer War of 1899-
1902!"

9.13 *German* (below)
"The Two Neptunes"
Roosevelt and Churchill are
mocked for their inability to
prevent U-boat strikes.

10.1 *Belgian*
"We are going to work in Germany."
During the occupation of their countries French and Belgian workers often earned higher wages in Germany than at home.

10. Nazi Propaganda for Occupied Europe

10.2 *German*
Recruitment poster for service with the German army.

10.3 *Belgian*
An attempt to associate
service with the Nazis' with
Belgian history.

10.5 *Dutch*
Recruiting for the Dutch section of the Nazi Transport Corps: "You too belong to us".

10.4 *Belgian* (1944)
"This is Mr. Prikkeldraad (Barbed-wire) who just happened to be in Neimegen when his English friends bombed it." A series aimed at Allied sympathisers

149

10.6 *Belgian*
Poster issued by occupying
Germans after the disastrous
Anglo-Canadian raid on
Dieppe in 1942.

10.7 *Channel Islands* (1941)
A formal and effective warning by
the occupying Germans

BEKANNTMACHUNG:

FRANÇOIS SCORNET,
geb. 25-5-1919, zuletzt wohnhaft in
Ploujean (Departement Finistère) ist
wegen Begünstigung des Feindes durch
beabsichtigte Unterstützung Englands
im Kriege gegen das Deutsche Reich
durch das Kriegsgericht

ZUM TODE

verurteilt und am 17-III-1941
erschossen worden.

Das Kriegsgericht.

Den 23-III-1941.

PUBLICATION:

The population is herewith notified, that
FRANÇOIS SCORNET,
born on May 25th 1919, residing in
Ploujean (Department Finistère) has
been sentenced

TO DEATH

by the German War Court and has
been shot on March 17th, 1941. This
had to be done, because of his favouring
the actions of the enemy by wilfully
supporting England in the war against
the German Empire.

German War Court.

March 23rd, 1941.

THE STAR, GUERNSEY, SATURDAY, SEPTEMBER 26, 1942

LA GAZETTE OFFICIELLE

BEKANNTMACHUNG

ALLE PERSONEN, DIE FUER MITTWOCH, DEN 23. SEPTEMBER 1942, ZUR EVAKUIERUNG BEORDERT WAREN, HABEN SICH NUNMEHR AM SONNTAG, DEN 27. SEPTEMBER 1942, ZU DEN IN DER ORDER ANGEGEBENEN ZEITEN AN IHREN SAMMELPLSETZEN ZUM ABTRANSPORT EINZUFINDEN.

DER FELDKOMMANDANT
gez. KNACKFUSS
Oberst.
GUERNSEY, SEPTEMBER 26, 1942.

NOTICE

ALL PERSONS WHO WERE NOTIFIED FOR WEDNESDAY, 23rd SEPTEMBER 1942, FOR EVACUATION, HAVE NOW TO REPORT ON SUNDAY, 27th SEPTEMBER, 1942, AT THE TIMES MENTIONED IN THE ORDER AT THEIR ASSEMBLING PLACES FOR EMBARKATION.

10.8 *Channel Islands* (1942) German proclamation seized during a small-scale raid on Sark in 1942.

10.9 *French* (1941) Another German announcement of the execution of a resistance fighter.

Bekanntmachung

Der Kraftfahrer
Robert DEREGNAUCOURT

wohnhaft in Paris, ist wegen Gewalttat gegen einen Angehörigen der deutschen Wehrmacht durch das Kriegsgericht zum

TODE

verurteilt und am
10. Januar 1941
ERSCHOSSEN worden

Den 11. Januar 1941. **Das Kriegsgericht.**

ARRÊT
de la Cour Martiale

Pour avoir commis des **actes de violence contre un militaire allemand**, le nommé:

Robert DEREGNAUCOURT
Chauffeur

domicilié à Paris, a été condamné à la

PEINE DE MORT
Il a été
FUSILLÉ
le 10 Janvier 1941

Fait le 11 Janvier 1941. **La Cour Martiale.**

151

10.10 *Greek* (1944)
A German announcement
that, because of the work of
Communist agitators,
anyone found within a
certain distance of the
Athens-Lamia railway will
be "shot at without
warning."

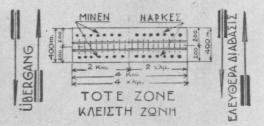

NIEDERLÄNDER!

Der Kampf im Osten ist für Euch kein Schauspiel, keine Störung Eurer Ruhe, sondern Euer Schicksal.

Tausende von jungen Niederländern haben dies schon erkannt, haben sich zu den Waffen gemeldet und kämpfen in dieser Stunde schon in den Reihen der deutschen Heere um den Bestand und die Zukunft Europas und damit des niederländischen Volkes.

Tausende sich ihrer Verantwortung für Europa bewusste Niederländer melden sich in den letzten Wochen und Tagen, um im Verein mit den Kampfgenossen aus Bulgarien, Dänemark, Deutschland, Finnland, Frankreich, Italien, Kroatien, Norwegen, Portugal, Rumänien, Schweden, Slovakei, Spanien und Ungarn als niederländischer Verband für die Verteidigung des Abendlandes und für ein einiges, starkes und friedensgesichertes Europa anzutreten. Für die Aufstellung des Verbandes hat sich Generalleutnant H. A. Seyffardt zur Verfügung gestellt. Ich entspreche diesem Wunsche und rufe alle einsatzbereiten Niederländer auf, im

Freiwilligen Legion Niederlande

gegen den Bolschewismus und für das eigene Volk und Vaterland zu kämpfen.

Der Reichskommissar
für die besetzten niederländischen Gebiete,
SEYSS-INQUART
Reichsminister

NEDERLANDERS!

De strijd in het Oosten is voor U geen schouwspel, geen verstoring van Uw rust, doch Uw lot.

Duizenden jonge Nederlanders hebben dit begrepen; zij zijn te wapen gesneld en strijden in dit uur reeds in de rijen van het Duitsche leger om het bestaan en de toekomst van Europa en daarmede van het Nederlandsche Volk.

Duizenden Nederlanders, zich bewust van hun verantwoordelijkheid voor Europa, geven zich in de laatste weken en dagen op, tezamen met hun strijdmakkers uit Bulgarije, Denemarken, Duitschland, Finland, Frankrijk, Italië, Kroatië, Noorwegen, Portugal, Roemenië, Zweden, Slowakije, Spanje en Hongarije, als Nederlandsche afdeeling voor de verdediging van het Avondland en voor een eensgezind en sterk Europa, waarin de vrede verzekerd zal zijn, aan te treden. Luitenant-Generaal H. A. Seyffardt heeft zich ter beschikking gesteld teneinde deze afdeeling samen te stellen.

Ik voldoe hierbij aan dezen wensch en roep alle Nederlanders, die zich willen inzetten, op om in het

Vrijwilligerslegioen Nederland

te strijden tegen het Bolsjewisme en voor Volk en Vaderland.

De Rijkscommissaris
voor het bezette Nederlandsche gebied,
SEYSS-INQUART
Rijksminister

10.11 *Dutch*
"Dutch people! The fight in the East is no spectacle, nor a disturbance to your peace, it is your fate." An attempt to whip up support for the war against bolshevism.

11. Resistance in Occupied Countries

INDIE MOET VRIJ !
WERKT EN VECHT ERVOOR!

11.1 *Dutch*
"The Indies must be freed"
(Pat Keely)
A British-produced poster calling for liberation of the Dutch East Indies from Japanese conquest. Note recurring octopus symbol (see 9.7).

153

11.2 *Canadian*
Supporting Dutch
Resistance.

11.3 *Dutch*
(Printed in Britain)

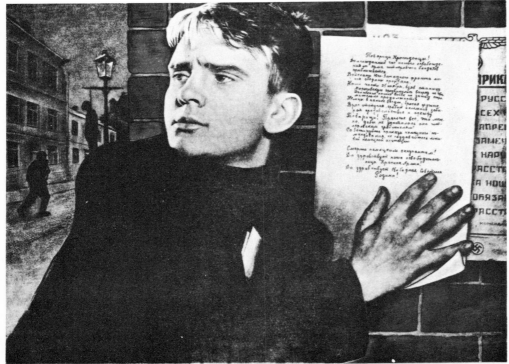

СЛАВА „МОЛОДОЙ ГВАРДИИ" КРАСНОДОНА!

В глубоком подполье шахтерского городна Краснодона была создана комсомольская организация „Молодая гвардия". Молодые сталинские орлята начали партизанскую деятельность, полную опасности и героизма. Выпускались листовки, сообщавшие о положении на фронтах, о победах Красной Армии. В дни советских праздников вывешивались красные флаги на деревьях, на домах Краснодона. Комсомольцы совершили поджог немецкой биржи, передавали еду заключенным в гестапо и деньги их семьям. Ногда презренные предатели выдали немцам „Молодую гвардию", герои-комсомольцы

стойно и мужественно выдержали жестокие пытки. С пением „Интернационала", измученные и связанные, но гордые и непокоренные, пошли они на казнь, полные ненависти к немецким палачам, полные веры в победу своего народа.

Организаторам „Молодой гвардии" Олегу КОШЕВОМУ, Сергею ТЮЛЕНИНУ, Ивану ЗЕЛЕНУХИНУ, Ульяне ГРОМОВОЙ и Любови ШЕВЦОВОЙ присвоено звание Героев Советского Союза. Их славные соратники по борьбе награждены орденами.

11.5 *Polish* (right)
(M. Zulawski)
(1939)
A British based
fund.

11.4 *Russian*
(V. Koretsky)
"Praise to the
'Young Guard' of
Krasnodon."
A tribute to the
resistance in a
small Russian
town.

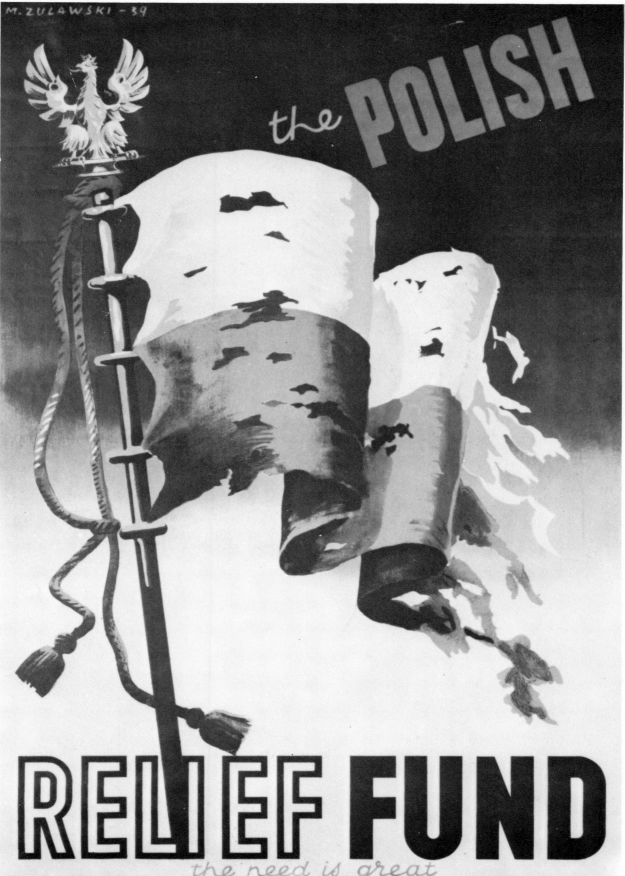

ЧТО С ВОЗА УПАЛО—

ТО ПРОПАЛО!

EN AFRIQUE
EN FRANCE
PARTOUT

UN SEUL COMBAT
POUR UNE SEULE PATRIE

11.6 *Russian* (above left)
"What has fallen out of the cart is
lost." (Russian proverb.)

11.7 *French* (above right) (Knopf)
"In France, in Africa, Every-
where. One fight for one country."
A Free French poster, printed in
Britain.

A toute heure du jour, les chasseurs britanniques
effectuent des balayages au-dessus de la France occupée,
acclamés par les paysans français

11.8 *French*
"At all hours of the day British
fighters carry out sweeps over
occupied France, to the cheers of
the French peasants."
Free French poster.

11.9 *Chinese*

11.10 *French* (Allyn Cox)
Printed in Britain.

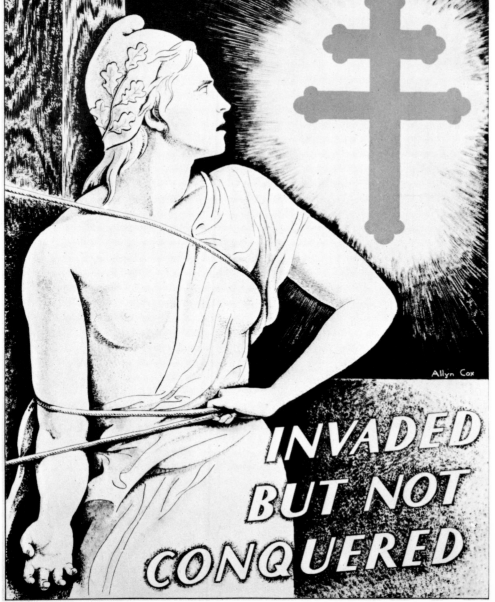

11.11 *Polish*
Printed in
liberated Italy.

11.12 *Philippino*
Printed in the
United States. An
attempt to stiffen
resistance in the
Philippines.

12. Epilogue

British   159

Index to Posters

Acknowledgements

The author and publishers wish to thank the following for their kind permission to reproduce photographs in this book: *Colour* – The Imperial War Museum, C.2–16, 18–22, 24–27, 30–36; Linda Cicalese, C.17, 23, 28; Musée Royale de l'Armée, Brussels, C.29; *Black and white* – The Imperial War Museum, 1.2–13, 1.15, 2.5–7, 2.10–12, 2.14, 2.15, 2.17, 2.22–29, 2.32–35, 2.37–4.5, 4.7, 4.9–12, 4.17, 5.1, 5.4–12, 5.14–18, 5.20–22, 5.24–28, 6.2–7, 7.4–6, 8.4, 8.6, 8.8–9.6, 9.8, 9.9, 9.13, 10.2, 10.4–5, 10.7–11.1, 11.3–12, Epilogue; Lords Gallery, 1.1, 2.4, 5.13, 7.3, 9.7, 11.2; The Hiroshima Peace Memorial Museum (and Mr. Yoshiteru Mizuma), 1.14, 2.8, 2.9, 2.18, 5.3, 5.23 (and Mr. Shozo Sugihara), 4.13; Pictorial Press Ltd., 2.3, 2.30, 4.15, 4.16, 5.19, 5.29; Wiener Library, 2.1, 2.13, 2.16, 2.19–21, 4.6, 4.14, 8.1–3, 8.7, 9.11–12, 10.3; Musée Royale de l'Armée, Brussels, 2.36, 8.5, 10.1, 10.6; Stuart Durant, 4.8, 5.2, 6.1, 9.10. Other pictures appearing in the book are the property of the Wayland Picture Library.